Henry L. A. Culmer

The Resources and Attractions of Utah as they Exist Today

Set Forth for the Enquiring Public, Especially for the Midwinter Fair...

Henry L. A. Culmer

The Resources and Attractions of Utah as they Exist Today
Set Forth for the Enquiring Public, Especially for the Midwinter Fair...

ISBN/EAN: 9783337250911

Printed in Europe, USA, Canada, Australia, Japan

Cover: Foto ©Andreas Hilbeck / pixelio.de

More available books at **www.hansebooks.com**

The Resources and Attractions of Utah

1894.

THE
Resources and Attractions

— OF —

UTAH

AS THEY EXIST TODAY.

SET FORTH FOR THE ENQUIRING
PUBLIC, ESPECIALLY FOR

THE · MIDWINTER · FAIR,

CALIFORNIA, 1894.

COMPILED BY H. L. A. CULMER

FOR THE

Midwinter Fair Committee

and the Salt Lake Chamber of Commerce.

PRINTED BY
GEO. Q. CANNON & SONS CO.
Salt Lake City,
1894.

UTAH.

UTAH occupies an important position in the trans-Mississippi group of states. It adjoins Colorado, Nevada, Arizona and Idaho. It is 275 miles in width and 345 miles in length. The splendid Wasatch Mountains sweep down its center and the Uintah Mountains cross its upper half. It is a region of snow-clad mountains and broad beautiful valleys. A hundred streams flow from the mountains and meander through the vales. It has a number of fresh water lakes of considerable size, and that wonderful inland sea, the Great Salt Lake, is a far-famed feature of its topography. Within the border lines of the Territory there exists a most remarkable variety of country, containing many unique features, and some that have made it world-famous, such as the grand canyons of the Colorado, and other wild scenery of the southern portion of the Territory. Lying between lofty mountain ranges are beautiful and verdant valleys, capable of susta:ning a very large population, and affording a variety of scenery that makes the whole Territory singularly attractive and a charming place of abode. A greater portion of its area constitutes the eastern and fruitful portion of the Great Basin,—that strange region whose waters are lost in the earth and never reach the ocean. The eastern half of the Territory is drained into the Colorado. The population of Utah is about 235,000; its area is 87,730 square miles. The mountain chains usually run north and south, and nearly all of them contain zones of precious metals. Probably no other state in the Union contains within its borders such a variety of resources. No other state could be so nearly independent and self-supplying. If intercourse were totally cut off from the outside, there are very few of the necessaries or luxuries of life that could not be produced within the boundaries of Utah in abundance. It is an empire within itself. This fact will be easily realized by a study of the endless variety of products described in this account. Although it is less than fifty years since settlement began in this Territory, the extraordinary scope of our possibilities in mining, agriculture, industry, in ranch and range production, and internal commerce already developed, proves this beyond question; and much of what is now imported might easily be produced in our midst, should it become necessary. With every variety of climate, which is generally salubrious and agreeable, there are the valleys for the farmer, the gardener and the fruit grower; the foot hill slopes and terraces for the sheep raiser; the mountains for the miner; the scenery and hunting among the mountains, the water fowl and grouse of the prairies for the pleasure seeker; the thermal springs, the Salt Lake air and bathing for the invalid, and plenty of opportunity and occupation for the man of business and enterprise.

CLIMATE AS A RESOURCE.

The wonderful climate of Utah has received the attention of some of the best writers on the subject in America, and in many very important features it has been acknowledged to approach the "ideal climate,"—a treasure that has been sought as eagerly as any boon which the world offers. To be thorough in recording, however briefly, extracts from the leading articles that have been published on the climate of Utah Territory, we must refer to the testimony of Father Silvestre Velez de Escalante, the first white man to set foot on Utah's soil, who started from Santa Fe and reached Utah Lake on the 23rd of September, 1776, and thereupon inscribed upon his tablets, that "Here the climate is so delicious, the air so balmy, that it is a pleasure to breathe it by day and by night."

From the voluminous writings of such eminent resident physicians and climatic students as Drs. Standart, Hamilton, Bascom and Niles, and other writers, we gather these undisputed facts regarding the air we breathe and the health-giving qualities of the climate of this Territory.

We have in Utah, or more particularly, in the Great Salt Lake Basin, a climate peculiarly local, and of a quality conducive to good health and long life. It possesses the dryness, elevation and tonicity of the air essential to the comfort and enjoyment of the hale as well as to the restoration of the invalid.

Added to the other manifold blessings enjoyed by those who dwell amid the valleys and mountains of Utah, they can, when in health, work harder and accomplish more with less wear and tear than anywhere else on the habitable globe. With a fair endowment of brains and working capital they can think faster; with brawny arms and inherent energy they can expend more force with less fatigue, and render by sundown a day and a quarter for a day's work without unusual effort. They can eat and assimilate more, and sleep better in Utah than the average man elsewhere; in brief, under the stimulus of local conditions of climate, they can return—other things being equal—in thought and force, more and better work than the average of mankind in less fortunately endowed localities. The property of exhilaration, born of purity and rarity of our atmosphere, is an ever constant factor. Coming here from other localities, there is an increase in the force of circulation and in the normal oxidation of the blood, together with a stimulus of the respiratory sense, and general improvement in the body nutrition. The summer heat is not debilitating. The dry, pure air and the cool invigorating nights enable us to maintain health throughout the year. Indeed, as a people we can retire to refreshing sleep to waken with renewed life and energy to begin another day prepared for the grand struggle of life. The people of Utah are as robust and long-lived as any in the world.

No region excels ours in natural advantages for the well-being of its citizens. We have a great inland sea rolling at our feet possessing inherent virtues in its waters essentially tonic and invigorating to the general system. We have thermal springs of varying degrees of temperature and of varied properties; we have the sunshine peculiar to a dry climate and we thrive upon it; the sunshine coming to us through a clear pure atmosphere reflects cheerfulness and makes the world smile. We live in nature's sanitarium subjected to healthful influences and dwelling under a cloudless sky. Our most favorable climatic properties are dryness, coolness and equability. Dr. Standart claimed our ideal climate to consist in the varied topography of this inter-mountain region. The cool fresh air of the mountains, light and pure; the peculiar local atmosphere of the Great Salt Lake; the distance inland; the sheltered situation of our valleys; their elevation above sea level, all combining to create what many travelers have found here, "the most unique and wonderful climate on the face of the globe."

We have no cyclones, blizzards, sand-storms, tornadoes nor earthquakes. The velocity of the wind is less in winter than in summer. This is true of no other place in the United States, except San Francisco. The average velocity of the winds per hour is 5.2 miles. In Boston it is 9.2; in Sandusky, Ohio, 12.8; St. Louis, 9.8; Cheyenne, 10.6; Denver, 6.3; San Francisco, 9.3. High winds are very rare, the highest velocity on record in Salt Lake City being but 48 miles per hour. In many eastern cities it reaches 60 and 70 miles per hour quite frequently. There are no damp winds. The relative humidity is 48.3 as against Los Angeles 66, New York 68. Therefore a low temperature is not uncomfortably cold or penetrating, and a high temperature is not oppressive. Sunstrokes are unknown, malaria is extremely rare, and the winter days, however cold, are invigorating. The highest temperature on record was in August, 1875, 101 degrees, the average highest temperature for fourteen years being 96 degrees. But the dry and absorbent nature of the air moderates the effect of such hot days. In autumn, the climate of Utah is simply unapproachable in all the qualities that make weather delightful,—clear, sparkling and bracing. From September until Christmas the sun shines perpetually, and out-door exercise is delightful. The annual average mean range of temperature is

51.5; the average monthly range is 47.5, and the average daily range is 18.6. This means that we have winter and summer; the seasons make their rounds; we have snow-fall and frost, sleighing and skating in winter, showers and blossom-time in spring, warmth and fruitfulness in summer, and bracing, open weather in the autumn. This is not a country where the weather is mild all the year; we have the changing seasons, the real summer and the real winter, which is desirable. Professor Jones says: "It is undoubtedly true that a climate where there is no difference between Christmas and the 4th of July, where every day is like every other, except for the dust, is a first-class place to die in; but to live, we want a climate that will stir up our energies, that will bring out all our powers and keep us alive and aggressive, without making us suffer because of its rigor; this we have in Utah." The records show that the extreme yearly range of our temperature is oftener less than 90 degrees than it is more than 100 degrees. It has exceeded 100 degrees but three times in twenty-four years. At Montreal the annual range is 140; New York City, 114 degrees; St. Louis, 113 degrees; Chicago, 132 degrees; Denver, Colorado, 126 degrees.

But the pride of our climate and the feature in which it excels all others in America, is its equability. There is no other region as dry and as elevated as this where the daily range of temperature is so small. Equability has been regarded as belonging exclusively to low and moist localities, and variability as a distinguishing attribute of all high and very dry places. The valleys of Utah range from 4300 to 6000 feet in altitude, but higher altitudes are in easy reach by ascending any one of the hundreds of beautiful canyons that abut upon the valleys. It has been clearly pointed out that bacteria breeding disease exist in the greatest number at low altitudes, and at high elevations they do not live. The dryness is about the same as Denver, but the daily range of temperature is much less than in any other elevated regions, at least in the United States. It is not the cold winter time nor the hot summer-time that try the health of human beings, but it is the sudden and extreme changes of temperature that are so hard to bear, and which wreck the health. The signal service stations have a flag to be displayed when violent and extreme changes of temperature are approaching, so that people who know the danger of such extreme changes, may take the necessary precautions to protect themselves; but in Utah this flag is never used. It takes several days for the temperature to change 40 degrees, while there are places in the East where such a change takes place in an hour or two. There is scarcely any dew in this country, so that the nights are as dry as the days. We have no rainy season, but we have showers all through the summer. We have no fogs nor drizzling rains, nor fierce and cold winds, and on the average 315 days out of the year are clear

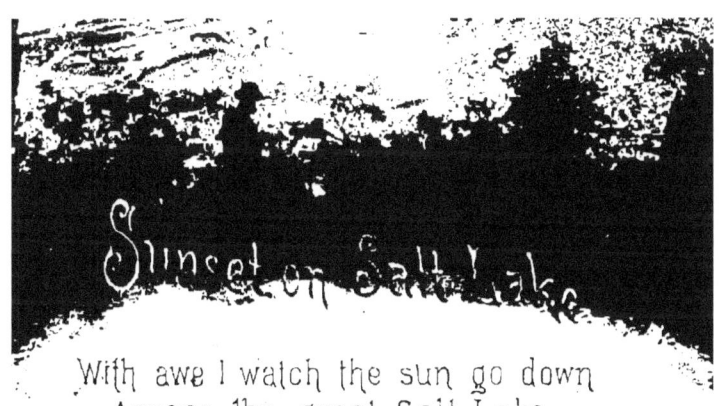

Sunset on Salt Lake

With awe I watch the sun go down
  Across the great Salt Lake,
The mountains don their golden crown,
The soaring seagulls circle 'round,
  The gentle billows break.

And when I scan what's made for man,
  To make his heart grow glad.
With wonderment my heart I hush;
I feel the flush of shame's hot blush,
  Because my soul is sad.

and fair. The average date of first snow in the valleys is November 1st. It never snows later than the middle of April. The first frost comes towards the end of September, and there is none later than April.

Dr. Niles says: "The physiological action of the climate is that of a strong stimulant tonic to the whole constitution, and especially to the nervous system. It is difficult for one who has never experienced the effects by coming from a low to a very high place, to understand the wonderful exhilaration that follows breathing this dry, rarified air. Those in health feel and enjoy the powerful tonic—almost intoxicating—effect, but not to the marked degree that the invalid does. It seems to supply a necessity in his case; nor are the effects limited to a temporary stimulant, to be followed by a corresponding depression. Very soon his appetite is better, his digestion improves, the feeling of lassitude disappears, exercise becomes a pleasure and he is able to enjoy the out-door life to which he is invited by new scenes, sunny skies and bracing air. With the increased exercise there is a more rapid gain in weight and strength.

"Dryness, equability, plenty of sunshine, absence of high winds, and coolness are all valuable and necessary high-altitude climatic features, and no place should be chosen where these conditions do not exist. But it is undoubtedly the stimulus of the lessened atmospheric pressure that exerts the most profound influence, and more than anything else it is the adaptation of this factor to the needs of the patient that decides the result."

W. Everett Smith regards sudden and violent daily ranges in temperature and high per cent. of relative humidity as the chief atmospheric conditions modifying health and therefore causing disease. The abundance of sunshine characteristic of high altitude places, aside from permitting and encouraging much-to-be-desired outdoor life, has a direct salutary effect upon the health and spirits of the invalid.

Dr. Thomas J. Mays states: "It may be truthfully said that there is no other element in our environment which modifies the bodily structure more palpably than mountain elevation. This influence pertains especially to the respiratory organs, and is principally, if not entirely, exerted by the thinness or attenuation of the atmosphere and by a diminution of air pressure on the outside of the body. It is estimated that at an elevation of 6000 feet the air contains about 25 per cent. less oxygen than it does at the seashore, and that the body is relieved of nearly 7000 pounds of outside pressure. Hence, ascending into a rarified environment the pulse is accelerated from fifteen to twenty beats per minute, the respiration is quickened in order to obtain the required amount of oxygen, and evaporation from the skin and lungs is increased. Protracted residence in such a region enlarges the chest capacity to a marked extent."

Physicians recommend this climate particularly for those suffering from pulmonary diseases, which cannot exist here except in a relieved and modified condition. Dr. Niles has covered this feature thoroughly, not only by his own extended observations, but by conference with others. He states: "The most rapid and satisfactory results have been noticed in that largest class of American invalids whose deteriorated health and loss of nervous, mental and physical vigor has been caused by overwork, worry, mental strain, etc., and which, without any recognizable specific cause, exhibit various distressing symptoms or functional disorder, such as neuralgias, sleeplessness, dizziness, mental depression, weak digestion, disturbance of the circulation, etc.

"As might naturally be expected, these troublesome patients usually respond promptly to the pleasant and complete change and to the invigorating influence of this climate.

."It is in the preventative and curative treatment of diseases of the respiratory tract, however, that this climate has attracted the most attention, and, perhaps, deserves the greatest credit.

"Chronic catarrhs of the nose, throat and bronchial tubes are favorably influenced from the first, but it is in the earlier stages of phthisis that the greatest power of these natural therapeutic agents are manifested. Many authentic instances are recorded where the progress of the disease has been checked (even after cavities have been formed or repeated hemorrhages have occurred) and the patient's general health restored. Some of the leading insurance companies realizing these facts take some risks (who have a tendency to lung trouble) on condition that they maintain a residence here.

"Visitors from a lower altitude suffering from asthma are usually promptly relieved by a residence here. Those suffering from chronic rheumatism, unless complicated by valvular deposits, are improved by the use of the springs, aided by the tonic air. The good results observed in all of those maladies dependent upon passive congestion of any of the internal organs (liver, kidneys, uterus, brain, etc.) are doubtless in a large measure due to the potent influence of the lessened atmospheric pressure in strengthening and equalizing the blood circulation, and the alterative effects of the sulphur springs water. This high, dry, cool air is unfavorable for the production and development of germ diseases, and this city is freer from these diseases than other cities of the same size."

The pure sparkling water which flows from the snow beds on the mountain ranges has much to do with preserving the health of our citizens, as there is no possibility of its contamination such as takes place in the large slow-flowing rivers of most other countries. The beneficial effects of our mineral springs and of bathing in the Great Salt Lake are referred to elsewhere.

AGRICULTURE.

It will be difficult to treat of this subject without conveying the impression that the writer suffers from chronic enthusiasm and cannot describe any resource of the Territory without resorting to the superlative, but no statements will be made in these pages which cannot be verified by undisputed evidence. It is not everything that can be grown in this Territory. Bread fruit, bananas, mangoes, sago and other tropical fruits or products cannot be produced. Oranges, figs and lemons can only be grown in the southern part of the Territory; but the agricultural products of Utah are wide in their range and almost without exception they are of excellent quality. Although our farms are small, we grow enormous crops to the acre. The expense per acre is large, but the yield compensates for the cost. Nearly all our farming requires irrigation, which almost doubles the labor otherwise required upon a crop, but irrigation means high cultivation, and it is therefore possible to produce from fifty acres as much as one hundred acres elsewhere would yield, so that a given area will support a larger farming population in this Territory than in other places. The soil is usually magnificent; charged with natural fertilizers, rich, deep and vigorous, seeming anxious to respond to the efforts of the husbandman when once the life-giving waters are spread upon its surface. There has never been a ton of artificial fertilizer brought to this Territory to our knowledge. The soil is charged with calcium-phosphate and other chemicals which nature requires to invigorate and sustain the fruits of the field. That subtle something which replaces the missing ingredients in the soil, is supplied in the waters of irrigation.

This is being more and better appreciated as time goes on. Alkali lands are caused from an excess of plant food, and they are becoming so understood. Granite, feldspar, porphyry and limestone, of which the mountains are formed, are prolific sources of potash and soda. Carbonate of lime, also essentially a plant food, and ammonia are both abundant.

The cultivated districts of Utah are in the valleys and lie between the mountain ranges throughout the whole of the Territory. It is true that in the western parts there are so-called desert regions, but so much has been done in the past few years to conquer the deserts of the Great Basin, and so many instances are at hand where lands once desert are now yielding abundant crops, that it is not safe to say that any land in this Territory is truly of a desert nature. The drive-well has invaded the arid regions, and wherever its waters can be made to flow, there the land makes most bountiful returns and yields up the substance of the field. Farming in Utah, however, seems to require more thought and ingenuity than elsewhere, but with these given, the response is greater. The quality of the product is, in many instances, beyond comparison with any other, not always as to appearance, but usually as to real merit and fine flavor. A review of the reports from the different counties of the Territory, as published in the later pages of this work, will show the astonishing variety of agricultural products produced in each county of Utah; and it will be further noted that the range of products is different in the southern counties to that of the northern.

These are the general facts regarding the agriculture of this favored Territory, but some remarkable and unique features will be noted in the detailed accounts which follow.

GRAIN.

Wheat.—The soil and climate of Utah is well adapted to the cultivation and growth of wheat. The latest official returns, gathered, however, with great care and accuracy, showed an average yield per acre of twenty-two bushels in 1890. The United States report for the same year shows 17.2, and the Agricultural College report shows an average from irrigated lands to be twenty-nine bushels in 1891. The United States report is not likely to be true, as the returns are gathered with far less completeness than the others. Our Territorial statistics of 1890, twenty-two bushels, is likely to be the nearest estimate to the truth. The real quality of the grain is equal to that of any grown in America, but in appearance it is not so plump as that of California, though brighter and larger than most wheat grown in the east. There is no steady export of Utah wheat, but occasionally we send it to Colorado and further east, and have more than once exported to England. The annual production approaches three million bushels. Sanpete and Cache Counties lead in production, closely followed by Utah, Weber and Salt Lake Counties. The price rarely falls below sixty cents, and frequently reaches seventy-five and eighty cents. Utah wheat exhibited by the Agricultural College of Logan, received an award at the World's Fair. Under our system of irrigation and consequent high cultivation the yield per acre in exceptional instances has been astonishingly great. In 1889 the American Agriculturist offered a prize of $500 to the farmer raising the largest crop of wheat to the acre in any place in the United States. This prize was secured by William Gibby, who produced 4806 pounds of clean wheat, being eighty bushels and six pounds, from one acre of ground, accurately surveyed, on the outskirts of Salt Lake City. The crop came up in the middle of February, 1889, and received no attention until April 10th, when it was rolled once. No other care was given it until harvest time, and the prize acre received no different treatment than the general wheat crop on the farm, the entire yield of which averaged seventy bushels to the acre. One bushel and one peck of seed was sown to the acre. The only fertilizer used was good stable manure. Careful farmers have kept a record of their time actually employed in wheat raising and have found that they have been able to make as high as ten dollars a day for the season. There are a number of small farms throughout Utah that have produced as high as sixty bushels to the acre year after year.

BARLEY FIELD, OGDEN VALLEY.

Some attention has recently been given with great success, to the growth of Egyptian seven-headed wheat, which yields sixty to seventy bushels to the acre, with comparatively little care.

Oats.—Those who keep up work horses are willing to pay twenty-five to thirty per cent. more for Utah oats of ordinary quality than for a fair grade of Eastern. Utah oats, therefore, command a good price, and when the market favors export a comparatively high figure is asked and received. The grain is handsome, heavy and full of meat. We have some 35,000 acres of oats under cultivation with an average yield of thirty-four bushels per acre, worth six hundred thousand dollars. Utah County produces the greatest quantity and Box Elder County stands first in the average yield per acre, producing fifty bushels to the acre in 1890. Large farms have been known to realize eighty-five bushels to the acre. Although last year's yield was rather less than usual, we have authentic instances of from seventy to eighty bushels to the acre.

Barley.—There was no barley exhibited at the World's Fair equal to that produced in Utah. Our barley has always been considered superior to any other produced in the United States. It is very heavy,—fifty to fifty-five pounds to the bushel, thin-

WHEAT FIELD. BOUNTIFUL, DAVIS COUNTY. 60 BUSHELS PER ACRE.

skinned and in every way superior. The white club variety is largely grown for brewing purposes and is in demand throughout the East in competition with the best Canadian. Several train loads have been exported this season to Cincinnati and other eastern points. The annual crop approximates half a million bushels, the largest product being in Utah County. Some of the southern counties produce the highest average to the acre, that of Garfield County fifty-two bushels in 1890. The price is usually about fifty cents per bushel. Utah's average per acre is 7.3 bushels greater than the average for the United States.

Corn.—Although Utah does not pose as a corn country, there are nearly ten thousand acres under cultivation. The hot sultry nights which corn requires are not characteristic of our climate, but in some of the southern parts excellent crops are produced.

Rye.—Comparatively little is cultivated in Utah, although the quality is superb and the yield above that of the aveiage for the United States.

GRASSES.

Alfalfa.—This is one of the most important crops of Utah. It can be grown on rough ground that is too dry for grass and too broken and stony for grain. The cultivation of alfalfa, or lucern, has proven one of the greatest blessings enjoyed by the farming people of Utah. Excellent crops have been secured by merely clearing off the brush and casting the seed over the ground. It takes longer to get a good start this way, and it is more difficult than if the ground is stirred or broken, but it thrives better in the end. Alfalfa will do well on ground that is too steep for a mowing machine if only sufficient water can be got to it to give it a start. Such land would require twenty-five pounds of seed for timothy, but for the raising of alfalfa, not over five pounds of seed is required. In the second year it will self-sow thinly. It does not thrive on cold and wet ground. The first season it should be cut as often as it is high enough to do so; the second crop will afford a little hay; the third cutting about half a crop, making about one whole crop for the season. The second year it will be as good as it ever becomes, and will give three strong crops, yielding on the average four or five tons to the acre. Sometimes eight tons per acre can be secured. The average in Emery County for 1890 was six tons to the acre. Utah County produces the greatest quantity, nearly fifty thousand tons. More or less alfalfa is grown in every county of the Territory. Probably one hundred and fifty thousand acres are now under cultivation. Alfalfa once planted, needs no re-sowing; it is cut each time when it is well out in blossom. In exceptional cases one seed has been known to throw out five hundred shoots, all that a strong man can lift. When left for seed it sometimes reaches a height of six feet. The quality of alfalfa seed raised in Utah is beyond comparison with that of any other region known. Many carloads are annually exported. In California and elsewhere there is a steady demand for it. Utah alfalfa seed secured first prize at the World's Fair, and this has done much to stimulate export trade during the past year. The market for this year makes the growing of alfalfa highly profitable. In the dry sand hills a good crop of lucern hay can be cut in June; then in the dry summer a lesser crop matures, which is harvested for seed, and being more sparsely grown than if irrigated, it is better for that purpose. A good average yield of seed from such lands would be six hundred pounds to the acre, worth about forty dollars. Alfalfa, like all other forage grasses, cures quickly in this climate and retains its color and flavor to a remarkable degree.

Hay.—Clover, timothy and red top hay are grown in all parts of the Territory. Hay cures beautifully and retains its nourishing quality better in this Territory than elsewhere, owing to the dry atmosphere. Morgan County in 1890 produced 3.2 tons on the average to the acre and the yield is probably as great as that of any district recorded in statistics. Cache County is a great hay producing region. Utah grasses exhibited at the

CELERY FIELD. OGDEN, WEBER CO.

World's Fair were pronounced beyond comparison with any others shown in the agricultural building.

Vegetables, etc.—The Utah potato is justly famous all over the United States. In 1890 there were some eight thousand acres under cultivation, yielding a million bushels; but that was an off year; our annual product is usually much greater. Utah County is the greatest producer, its average being one hundred and sixty-eight bushels in 1890; but it is not unusual for four hundred bushels of magnificent potatoes to be produced to the acre. As high as eight hundred and even nine hundred to the acre have been recorded. The late Secretary Rusk said, "Utah beats the world for potatoes.' The manufacture of starch from Utah potatoes would prove successful.

Utah has also a fine reputation for carrots, which sometimes yield, of good quality, as much as eighteen hundred bushels to the acre; also for onions, turnips, parsnips, radishes, etc. The great beet sugar factory at Lehi has developed the cultivation of sugar beets throughout the middle counties. Last year this factory consumed 26,800 tons of sugar beets, for which they paid $135,000. 2700 acres were under cultivation, by far the greatest number being in Utah County. A description of the beet sugar industry is given under the head of Utah County.

We annually export large quantities of cabbage, cauliflower and celery, the latter growing exceptionally fine; and for home consumption we raise an abundance of beans, peas, lettuce, cabbage, squash, tomatoes, asparagus, etc. In the production of these garden stuffs, Davis County takes the lead. Peanuts could be grown to advantage in this Territory, our climate and soil being especially favorable. Tobacco, flax, hops, sorghum and other miscellaneous crops have not been rightly cultivated but could be produced to advantage. In the southern part of the Territory, cotton is very successfully raised. It averages six hundred pounds to the acre, which is an enormous yield, the average for the southern states being usually about one hundred and seventy pounds.

THE ORCHARDS OF UTAH.

The same causes which give excellence to the grains and vegetables of Utah also stand for orchard products of a high class. Fresh fruits are exported in considerable quantities, and wherever sent take a high place and command a ready sale. In general terms, the superior characteristics are firmness, beauty, and above all, fine flavor.

Nearly every county in the Territory produces fruit, Utah County most of all; Box Elder, Weber and Davis following closely. In Washington County, figs, pomegranates, grapes and other semi-tropical fruits thrive to perfection, though they are too far from the railroads to meet with a ready market. With reasonable care, peaches are raised in all the lower altitude valleys to advantage. They are shipped wrapped and unwrapped, in boxes of about twenty pounds each, and find a ready market in Colorado and elsewhere. Our peach trees thrive best on light, loamy and gravelly soil. Apples are better and becoming more plentiful every year. Great quantities are raised in Weber and Utah Counties and shipped from Ogden, Salt Lake City, Provo and Springville to the markets of the east and north. Box Elder County also makes large shipments. The principal varieties for export are the fall Pearmain and Rhode Island

Greening; but among the last and very best to come into market are the Winesap and winter Pearmain, which keep far into April and are generally conceded to be of better flavor than those from the East.

Plums, German prunes, pears, apricots, cherries and grapes of splendid quality and handsome appearance are raised in great quantities; strawberries and raspberries are both native to Utah; also red and black currants; under cultivation the yield is very large and of surprising quality. In the height of the season, strawberries come to market in the greatest abundance, of magnificent appearance and fine flavor.

Reference to dried fruits will be found in the article on range products of Utah.

The value of the grain, grasses, vegetables and fruits produced in Utah in 1890 was computed by the Territorial statistition to be $8,309,705.80.

IRRIGATION.

THE farmers of Utah were the first to prove the advantages of irrigation in the arid regions of the United States. They believe in it and depend upon it, and in so doing they feel a sense of security and achieve results which fully compensate for the extra labor thus involved. In seasons of drouth, when the eastern farmer is praying for rain, those of Utah are turning on the water. According to the latest and most reliable data there were 374,340 acres of land under cultivation in the Territory, 310,759 of which were actually irrigated. Out of eleven thousand farms, about ten thousand depend upon irrigation; the remainder being either stock ranches or elevated districts where dry farming is practiced. Irrigated farms are usually small, averaging about thirty acres. There are only five irrigated farms in the Territory of six hundred and forty acres or upwards. The greatest number of irrigators are in Salt Lake County, but the greatest number of irrigated acres are in Cache and Sanpete Counties; Utah and Weber Counties following quite closely. Some of the largest farms are in Rich, and Uintah Counties, but they are not the greatest producers. The farms lying along the base of the Wasatch mountains, near the markets of the large cities, being smaller and more highly cultivated. The value of the products of some of these is remarkably great.

The average first cost of bringing water on to the land is about ten dollars per acre for the entire territory, and the average value placed by the farmer upon such water right is twenty-seven dollars per acre. The average annual cost of maintaining this water right throughout the Territory is ninety cents per acre. The average first cost of land and water is about twenty-seven dollars per acre; and the average annual value of

18   RESOURCES AND ATTRACTIONS OF UTAH.

production is eighteen dollars, as against thirteen dollars for New Mexico and fourteen dollars for Arizona. As compared with farms of surrounding states those of Utah are in a much higher state of cultivation. The cultivated areas are usually along the bases of the high mountain ranges, from which separate streams issue every few miles. They are thus favorably situated for cheap and effective irrigation and in the early part

FLOWING WELL, NEAR SALT LAKE CITY.

of the season when water is most plentiful it carries fertilizing elements that maintain the productiveness of the land. Experiments made by the Utah Agricultural College prove conclusively that irrigation streams possess more of the qualities nutritious to vegetation than are obtained from rain water. In all such districts, large areas of land are extremely productive and support a considerable farming population, with thrifty towns not far apart from each other. Utah occupies a central position in the arid region and its details of irrigation possess unusual interest; the farmers having introduced methods of their own and achieved success after repeated failures, they are now well able to instruct the rest of America in the art of irrigation. Until a year or two ago, no attempts had been made at diverting large streams for irrigation purposes, the capital required being greater than the farmers could gather together for the purpose; but in Sevier County the Swan Lake Reservoir and Canal Company has constructed a reservoir covering forty thousand acres, and built a large canal many miles in length to irrigate a tract containing some two hundred thousand acres of fertile land, which but for this enterprise could never be cultivated. In Parley's Park, in Goshen Valley and in other valleys, similar enterprises, on a smaller scale, however, are under way; but the greatest undertaking of this character is in Box Elder County, where the Bear River Canal, built at a cost of two million dollars, and having already seventy miles of main canal and one hundred and fifty miles of laterals, has been constructed, to bring under cultivation one hundred and fifty thousand acres of the choicest lands in Utah, which have hitherto been unoccupied and would have remained so but for this enterprise.

To a limited extent, farming in Utah depends on the amount of snow-fall in the mountains, but experience has shown that there is usually sufficient to irrigate nearly all of the land that is under cultivation, and plans can be made with confidence that the harvest will be sure. With experience and increase in the farming population, greater economy is being practiced and a given quantity of water is made to support larger areas of land. Potatoes, corn, vegetables and all plants growing in hills or rows are irrigated by furrows, the water flowing in small streams through the furrows and gradually moistening the ground on each side. Grain is usually watered by flooding; but more generally the ground is marked off by means of some simple contrivance made by the farmer. After grain is planted, the fields are sometimes rolled with a heavy roller having projections twelve to twenty-four inches apart, which makes small grooves in the surface of the field and in such a direction that there is a constant though gradual slope from one end to the other. The water is then let into these little markings or grooves the same as if they were furrows. When this is well done irrigation proceeds rapidly and with the least waste of water. Utah's irrigation model exhibited at the World's Fair was one of the most interesting features of the Agricultural Department.

It is probable that with great economy and by the storage of winter and surplus water a million acres might soon be irrigated in Utah. Natural storage basins or reservoirs exist in and around the higher mountains in nearly all parts of the Territory. Alpine lakes formed by glacial action exist near the heads of the canyons, and with little labor these could be converted into natural storage basins of enormous capacity. By these and other means it has been computed by Professor Jones that in Beaver County alone over two billion cubic feet of water could be saved for irrigation; in Garfield County, three billions;in Utah County there are seven valley sites and twenty-seven mountain sites capable of holding at least a billion feet; as large a quantity could be saved in Kane County, or Millard County; and no doubt there are many other districts in which improvements of this character could be made to advantage and the agricultural district largely increased. Enormous profits await those who engage with reasonable judgment in such enterprises.

IRRIGATED CABBAGE FIELD NEAR OGDEN, 8000 HEADS TO ACRE.

In the report from Wasatch County it will be noted that there are only eighteen thousand acres now irrigated, but that there is water enough to irrigate nearly twice as much.

A remarkable water supply—a great blessing to the farmers of Utah—has been obtained during recent years by drive wells. Of these there were some twenty-five hundred in 1890. The average depth is one hundred and forty-five feet, costing seventy-seven dollars per well, or about fifty cents per foot. They range from one and a quarter to four inches in diameter. The average discharge is twenty-six gallons per minute, but some of them are regular geysers and irrigate a considerable area. On the average they irrigate nearly five acres, and are chiefly used for watering market gardens. The wells are made by drilling and by driving pipe through the sand and clay until some pervious and water-bearing layer is reached. They range from thirty feet in depth on the lowest ground up to four hundred feet or more near the edge of the valley. The water thus produced is usually of excellent quality.

One only need traverse the rich ranges that rest along both flanks of the Wasatch and note the fertile character of the soil, to be convinced that only water service is needed to make vast tracts, now wholly unoccupied, become most attractive as well as productive. It must not be supposed that all the lands open for settlement lack water supply. In the rich benches of the water-sheds of the Uintah Mountains, and in the valley approaches there remain unfenced and unimproved large districts inviting to the plow and to which an ample water supply can be conveyed easily from unappropriated sources. Other tracts cannot be irrigated, yet make excellent grazing lands, while still others can be converted into fields and pastures if ever the government will reach forth its aid toward the building of reservoirs and canals, which settlers cannot think of contemplating at their own cost.

Of these lands, a considerable portion belong to the original land grant of the Union Pacific Railway represented in Salt Lake City by C. E. Wantland, and favorable terms are now being offered to settlers, the terms of payment being easy, and large concessions made to bona-fide purchasers who improve the country. Of such lands, no fewer than half a million acres of the most varied character are for sale in Utah alone; and from this area there are some desirable homesteads to be selected. Much of this, and still more of unoccupied government land subject to settlement is also within easy reach of the Rio Grande Western, which company, through its general passenger agent, J. H. Bennett, is now actively engaged in promoting the settlement of the unimproved lands of Utah.

MINING.

Active mining commenced in Utah in 1870, although some developments had been made in the Cottonwood districts during the previous year. From that time until the present this industry has proven the principal source of revenue to the Territory, and has contributed much to its prosperity. As early as 1872, the production amounted to $2,547,916, the following year it had increased to $4,523,497, the annual production steadily growing until it reached its climax in 1892, when the production of gold, silver, lead and copper had a seaboard value of $16,276,818.00. The output would have continued to increase year by year had not anti-silver legislation in Congress depressed prices and caused a number of properties to shut down. As a result, the output for 1893 was only $12,832,074.00, the falling off being in silver, lead and copper, while the production of gold increased over forty per cent. It has been one of the marvels of the past year or two that while the low prices on lead and silver threaten to destroy our metal mining industry, the wonderful gold discoveries promise to offset a great part of the injury. This is one of many instances that prove the vitality of this country and the diversity of its resources. We have so many different sources of revenue that we cannot develop them all fully at one time, nor can they all fail us at one time. Silver, lead, copper and gold to the value of two hundred millions have been produced in Utah in the last twenty-two years, but if silver production were stopped entirely this Territory would still be an important mineral country, for greater attention would then be given to the development of our bodies of gold, copper, lead, iron, zinc, cinnabar, tin, bismuth, cobalt, antimony, manganese and other metals known to exist in more or less abundance in various parts of the Territory, and to the singular variety of other valuable minerals we can produce. Aside from the deposits of precious metals, explorations of our mountains prove them to be a gigantic laboratory wherein Nature has worked with infinite cunning for countless centuries and stored up vast treasures from which manufacturing and commercial communities may draw their supplies of crude material. In this respect it has been truly said that no State in the Union posesses a more diversified or valuable store. Among the mountains and valleys are deposits of alum, asbestos, asphaltum, barytes, borax, hydraulic cements, chromium, clays, copperas, coal, mica, nitre, onyx, petroleum, phosphates, plumbago, precious stones, pyrites, salt, soda, sulphur, talc, thermal springs, whetstones, lithographic stone, slate, building and ornamental stones and marbles of great variety, and probably other minerals which no doubt exist in the portions of the Territory that have not been closely explored. Utah's collection of specimens of the various minerals of the Territory won the highest prize at the World's Fair and will be shown at the Midwinter Fair.

To give a complete account of the development and possibilities of each of these would require a volume of itself, but some idea of the mineral resources of Utah may be gathered by a brief reference to a few of the most important.

Coal.—Of the two principal coal fields that have been so far developed in this Territory, one is at Coalville, Summit County, the other in Emery County, extending from Castle Gate to Scofield. Last year, Coalville produced 49,080 tons, and Emery County 331,878 tons, while an unknown but considerable quantity was produced in other parts of the Territory. Splendid coal beds also exist in a number of the southern counties. Near Wales, in Sanpete County, mines producing excellent coal have

been in operation since 1855. Near Beaver, a five-foot vein of excellent coal has recently been discovered. Near Cedar City, in Iron County, at a point adjacent to the great iron mountains, good coal is cheaply mined. At Vernal, in Uintah County, an excellent quality is easily procured. This is in the extreme north-east corner of the Territory, and another coal field exists in the extreme south-west corner of the Territory, near New Harmony in Washington County. The value of the coal annually produced in Utah is one million dollars, but with opportunities for export, such, for instance, as will arise on the completion of the railway from Los Angeles, the quantity may be many times doubled, as with a coal area of not less than five thousand square miles, there is absolutely no limit to our capacity for production. When it is realized that there are no coal mines between Utah and the Pacific coast, and that we are well able to supply the entire California demand, the future for Utah coal seems to be very great. The quality of our coal is excellent, both for heating and steam-making, and being hard it is well adapted for transportation to long distances. At Castle Gate, Emery County, the Pleasant Valley Coal Company manufactured 16,730 tons of coke of good quality, which was used by the smelters near Salt Lake City.

Iron.—There are iron deposits that can be worked with profit in Cache, Weber, Wasatch, Salt Lake, Morgan, Juab, and many other counties of Utah, but the greatest of all is in Iron County, which possesses one of the most remarkable deposits in the world. Near Cedar City, is the Iron Mountain, computed to contain fifty million tons of fine iron ore. Prof. Newberry has said of this mountain: "The deposits of iron ore near Iron City in south-western Utah are probably not excelled in intrinsic value by any in the world. The ore is magnetite and hematite, and occurs in a belt fifteen or twenty miles long and three or four miles wide, along which there are frequent outcrops, each of which shows a length and breadth of several hundred feet of compact massive ore of the richest quality. There are certainly no other deposits to compare with them west of the Mississippi for the manufacture of pig and bar iron and steel, and it would be difficult to estimate the influence they would have on the industries of the Pacific Coast."

Another acknowledged expert has said: "Utah's iron resources must exceed those of any other section of the Union." All the iron ore so far mined in Utah has been red and brown hematite, of which some 12,000 tons are annually used for flux in the smelters, but when it is realized that the largest and best of our iron deposits are located close to great coal measures, it is safe to predict that the day will yet come when the iron and steel required in the western half of this country at least will be produced within the Territory of Utah. We shall have big blast furnaces and foundries, and the railroads of the west will be equipped with rails made of Utah steel; we shall make all the stoves, machinery, iron pipe, and miscellaneous ironware of the trans-Mississippi country. It would pay even now, but with the proposed railway connection to the southern part of the Territory, such enterprises will begin at once.

Sulphur.—Excellent sulphur mines exist in Washington County and in other parts of the Territory, but the important deposit is that owned by the Utah Sulphur Company at Cove Creek, Millard County. This surpasses any other deposit in the known world, the sulphur being far richer and more abundant than in Sicily, from which the world draws its greatest supply, One thousand tons were shipped in 1893 to St. Louis, Chicago, Omaha, Denver, Kansas City and Portland, Oregon; but the trade is increasing and the developments at the mines will now permit a much larger output. The present production is fifty tons per day, 98 per cent. pure. The milling capacity is thirty tons, with a subliming chamber producing one and a half tons of flowers of sulphur daily. The output will probably be much greater in the future. The shipping point is Black Rock, on the Union Pacific system. Pyrites of iron exists in Salt Lake and other counties, and it has been shown that sulphuric acid can be economically manufactured from it in this Territory.

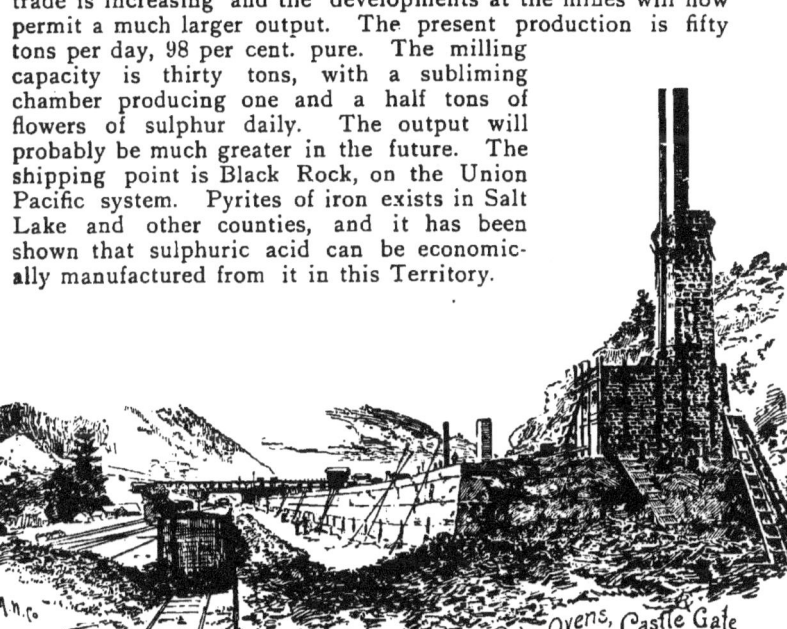

Coke Ovens, Castle Gate

Plaster of Paris.—At Nephi, Juab County, the Nephi Plaster Manufacturing Company supply the whole of Utah and ship large quantities to California. The output of 1893 was fifteen hundred tons, of superior quality. The raw material, gypsum, from which this is made, is said to be the purest known. The analysis is:

Lime	33.60
Sulphuric acid	43.07
Water	23.33
Total	100.00

This enterprise will probably develop into much greater proportions. An excellent exhibit is being prepared by the company for the Midwinter Fair.

Salt.—A company at Nephi, Juab County, is engaged in the manufacture of refined salt from the rock salt found near by, and another company is doing a large business in the sale of rock salt as mined. A number of the lower altitude counties of Utah can produce salt to advantage, epecially Sevier County; but the principal source of supply is in the Great Salt Lake itself, which is probably the best and largest deposit of brine in the world. Its waters carry about twenty per cent. of salt. Around the lake are salt farms, where ponds are made by building levees, to obtain salt by solar evaporation. This salt is stacked in piles and is ready for market as coarse salt for stock and for the amalgamating works throughout the mining regions. About one hundred thousand tons per annum are usually gathered in this way. The largest salt works are operated by the Inland Salt Company, in Salt Lake County, which employs a large number of men throughout the year. Crude salt for the silver mills brings $1.50 per ton on the cars, while the refined salt for dairy and domestic use brings about $12 per ton. The salt business of Utah amounts to about two hundred thousand dollars per annum.

Asphaltum.—The asphaltum fields of Utah are in the northeastern part of the Territory, almost the whole of Wasatch and Uintah Counties being impregnated with the mineral in a great variety of forms and conditions, the principal kinds being gilsonite, ozokerite (130,000 pounds produced in 1889), wurtzelite (often called elaterite), asphaltic limestone and gilsonite, which are the only forms that have been profitably worked. A combination of the two has been used successfully in paving the principal streets of Salt Lake City. The elastic quality of bitumen in this combination has made a desirable pavement pleasant to travel upon. It is comparatively noiseless. The asphaltum pavements laid in Utah have been done by the Wasatch Asphaltum Company of Salt Lake City, who operate their own mines in Utah and Wasatch Counties, and besides using a considerable quantity of asphaltum in this Territory, export a great many carloads every year to various parts of the United States. They also manufacture and ship mastic similar to the Val de Travers, and their "No. 1 Refined Asphaltum" takes the place of Trinidad for all purposes. The gilsonite shipped by them is superior to any other form of asphaltum produced in the world. It analyses 99.99 per cent. pure, while the next best, the Egyptian, is only 90 per cent. pure. All the largest varnish makers in the United States now use this form of Utah asphaltum for the manufacture of their highest grades of black Japans and asphaltum varnishes. All the black Japanned tin-signs used for gold lettering are prepared with it, and gilsonite is used also for all fine black varnish work, such as typewriters, bicycles, etc., to the exclusion of all other kinds. Gilsonite is produced only in Utah. In comparison with the Utah product, Trinidad asphaltum is a coarse article, being only thirty per cent. pure.

The veins from which gilsonite is mined are perpendicular fissures lying in horizontal strata of yellow sandstone. The shipping point is Price Station in Emery County. Several million pounds are exported annually to the best known varnish makers in the United States.

Gilsonite is also used to better advantage than any other material in the manufacture of roofing pitch, teredo-proof paints, first-class lubricants and insulating compounds. As an insulator it is the best material known. Tests by the Westinghouse Company have shown it to be a perfect insulator against the heaviest voltage which the largest electric plant in the United States can accumulate. At twelve hundred volts the insulation on a test piece one-eighth of an inch thick was perfect. It is used by the carload in the manufacture of insulated wire.

As a paving material the asphaltic limestone produced by the Wasatch Asphaltum Company has been demonstrated by practical proof in the laying of several miles of first-class pavement, to be the equal for this purpose of any asphaltum known. The production of asphaltum in Utah last year amounted to $150,000, and is likely to increase very rapidly in the near future.

Asbestos of good quality is found in Beaver County. Indications of *Petroleum* that are likely to lead to a profitable development are found in Emery County, near Pleasant Valley and near Green River. *Graphite* is discovered in Box Elder County and in Utah County. There are large beds not far from Provo and some near Goshen. One of the most remarkable deposits known of *Selenite* is found in Wayne County near the Fremont River. The crystals occur in a cave within a mound, from which have been taken prisms of perfect form from one to five feet in length and from ten to one hundred pounds in weight. This selenite is of perfect transparency, and the crystals are probably as magnificent as any that have ever been discovered. *Mica* is found in Box Elder County (see county article), in Davis County and Uintah County. The deposit in Box Elder County promises to furnish an article fit for commerce.

Clays.—A great variety of rich and beautiful clays exist in Utah, almost every county having a deposit of some kind of clay. In Salt Lake County, near Draper, is a vast bed of kaolin, from which articles of delicate and purest white pottery have been made on an experimental scale. At the base of the Wasatch mountains throughout Utah County is a deposit of black clay of the finest quality. Brick clays from which first-class brick are

MINING. 29

manufactured are found nearly everywhere throughout the Territory. The brick produced is of almost every color and tone. From our fire clays are produced a first-class quality of fire brick.

Veins carrying *bismuth* have been found in Beaver County near Beaver City, carrying from one to six per cent. of the metal. This metal has also been found in the mines of Bingham, but there are no reduction works in this country designed for its extraction.

Soda and *nitr* exist in Weber, Utah, and other Counties, and *alum* in abundance in Iron County.

Mineral Springs.—-It would be impossible to describe the mineral and thermal springs of Utah, so great are their variety and so widely scattered throughout the various counties. The best known are the sulphur springs on the outskirts of Salt Lake City, whose curative properties have aided the physicians in accomplishing wonderful restorations. The Idanha water of soda springs, near the northern boundary of the Territory, secured the first prize above every competitor at the World's Fair, rival waters being submitted from all parts of the world.

WASATKA WATER.

The greatest medicinal water which Utah presents today is the celebrated Wasatka mineral water, taken from springs on the northern outskirts of Salt Lake City. The marvelous health-giving and healing properties of this generous spring have only recently been brought on a large scale to the attention of invalids and others; but its reputation has spread rapidly and its curative powers are making it famous wherever it is used. Wasatka, or the "Milk Spring," derives its name from the peculiar soft or milk-like flavor. During the past two years many wonderful cures have been effected by this water, which has been proclaimed to be the finest remedy known for constipation and for disease of the kidneys and liver. Remarkable effects have followed its use as a remedy for abdominal obesity, indigestion, catarrh and insomnia. As a table water it is refreshing and invigorating. This seems a liberal statement to make regarding a mineral spring, but overwhelming testimony from physicians and their patients justify every assertion that is made. A recent exhaustive analysis by Walter S. Haines, Professor of Chemistry at the Rush Medical College, Chicago, made from samples of water, accompanied by an affidavit of J. P. Bache, Clerk of the Supreme Court of Utah, that it was taken direct from the Wasatka Springs, showed that each gallon contained:

	GRAINS.
Sodium Chloride	230.88
Potassium Chloride	3.06
Magnesium Chloride	21.24
Calcium Chloride	11.92
Lithium Chloride	0.12
Ammonium Chloride	0.25
Calcium Sulphate	59.50
Calcium Carbonate	4.75
Sodium Borate	traces
Magnesium Bromide	traces
Silica	0.75
Oxides of Iron and Aluminum	0.03
Total	332.50

In reference to the above one of our most prominent physicians has testified that this water could be safely recommended for general use. It is especially indicated in functional diseases of the digestive organs, liver and kidneys, on account of its alterative, aperient and diuretic effects.

For lead poisoning, rheumatism and some other diseases common in this section requiring drugs having special eliminating action, it is his opinion that Wasatka water would be beneficial.

The Wasatka Mineral Springs Company of Salt Lake City, Utah, bottle this water on a large scale, and not only find extensive demand for it throughout Utah, but are shipping it to considerable distances.

Other competent physicians have endorsed Wasatka water for various troubles, but the most remarkable claim made for it is that it is a cure for Bright's disease, and strong evidence has been given that this is perfectly true. The company offers evidence that should be convincing of the value of Wasatka water for the cure of this disease, and this alone should make it famous.

Building and Ornamental Stones.—The finest building stones of Utah are the gray freestone produced by the Kyune Graystone Company in Utah County. the gray and red sandstones produced by the Diamond and Kyune Company the granite of Little Cottonwood Canyon, Salt Lake County, and the oolite of Sanpete County. Of these, the gray kyune stone of which the city and county building is constructed in Salt Lake City is considered the favorite on account of its excellent texture, beautiful color and evenness. A further account of this stone will be found in the Utah County article. Kyune stone is so attractive and can be produced in such quantity that a large export trade will probably arise; and it is now proposed that a magnificent building about to be erected in San Francisco, in which a million and a quarter cubic feet will be used, will be constructed of kyune gray sandstone. Owing to its density and fine texture, it does not absorb moisture, a matter of little moment in this country, but of great importance in humid climates.

The white granite of Little Cottonwood has been used in the construction of the famous Salt Lake Temple, and the oolite of Sanpete County is the stone of which the beautiful Manti Temple is built.

Hard sandstone for flagging and foundations is found in many parts of the Territory, but the principal output is from the quarries of the Mountain Stone Company and the Metropolitan Stone Company and other quarries near Park City, Summit County. It is from this region that most of our pavements, sidewalks and stone steps are supplied.

Large deposits of fine marble of every hue are found in different parts of the Territory, from pure white statuary, half translucent, through every color and tone to jet black. Probably the largest deposit of white marble is that of the Wasatch Marble Company in Salt Lake County, the beds being forty to fifty feet in thickness and of splendid quality. It can there be more easily and cheaply produced than in Vermont, and must sooner or later attract the attention of capitalists. It is owned by Salt Lake parties. A handsome white and black marble is also found in American Fork Canyon, Utah County, where blocks of any desired size may be taken out. This marble is especially adapted for the construction of the fronts of buildings. In Cache and Box Elder Counties are also great varieties of marble, and excellent deposits of mottled red have been reported from Millard County, consisting of a ledge two hundred feet in thickness, by nearly five thousand feet in length. Other deposits are known to exist near Logan, Cache County, and a beautiful white carbonate of magnesia near Nephi, in Juab County. One of the best and most ornamental marbles, geodic in character, is found in Hobble Creek Canyon, Utah County. Being of a soft brown shade and susceptible of a fine polish, it is highly ornamental.

Much attention has been paid of late to the deposits of Mexican onyx existing in various parts of the Territory. North of Deseret, Millard County, Mr. R. A. McBride, of Paragonah, has unearthed a rich deposit which varies from rosewood to mahogany color, and in Box Elder County some beautiful varieties are being quarried for market; but the greatest development has taken place in the splendid deposits of Utah County, lying near the west shore of Utah Lake. The Mexican Onyx Company and some Lehi parties are separately working these deposits. The products are of infinite variety and as beautiful as any that have ever been sent to market. Pieces four by six feet are easily taken out, and can be cut and polished at a low cost. Some fifteen men are employed in the development of these quarries, and a number of carloads have been shipped to the east.

Slate for roofing and serpentine for mantel pieces and similar purposes, are found near Provo, in Utah County, of as fine a quality as that imported from Wales. It has no equal in America. A finer grade of slate suitable for razor hones is found in the mountains west of Lehi, in Utah County, and in Millard County a fine grained whetstone is to be had. The kyune graystone is well adapted for the manufacture of grind-stones.

Discoveries of *Lithographic stone* have been made in various parts of the Territory, but so far none has been marketed. Millard, Utah and Salt Lake Counties each claim to possess deposits of superior quality. Near Cisco, in Grand County, the West American Agate Company have been operating the agate fields and have spent some six thousand dollars in development. Large boulders of *Chalcedony*, big enough to make table tops, are there found ranging in color from bloodstone to carnelian.

COMMERCE.

The commerce and trade of Utah are confined to no limited field, but embrace within certain proportions nearly all the varied interests that belong to the country at large. In these matters, as in most others, while the proportions of our operations may not be so great as to excite wonder and admiration, it must be admitted that in point of variety no other State or Territory can view us with disdain. We have examined into the commercial activities of many States separately, and have been struck with the prevailing feature that each State, as a general proposition, maintains its activity in special lines, but in Utah this is not the case. The range of subjects which the man of trade in this Territory is called upon to consider is bewildering, and as varied as the numberless resources, mineral, agricultural and industrial, that are briefly referred to in these pages. If each of these interests can be developed, as we believe they will be, in proportion to their merits and the opportunities that exist in this Territory, the future of trade and commerce in the years to come will be exceedingly great. The demands of an active people, somewhat lavish in their requirements, endowed with energy, and learning to demand the luxuries as well as the necessaries of life, call for an increasing supply of the staples that engage the attention of commerce in every country. Not judging of trade by fluctuations in prosperity which affect every country, but marking the progress of commerce by years instead of by months, the trade of the whole Territory has increased steadily, until the volume of today bears an astonishing relation to that of a few years ago. This results principally from the fact that year in and year out, with as little oscillation as obtains in any other region, the Territory has enjoyed a continuous run of

COMMERCE.

comparative prosperity for a great number of years. We do not wish to repeat our statements, but we cannot refrain from claiming that this is essentially due to the variety of means by which the well-being of the residents of Utah can be sustained. It is only necessary to peruse these pages with a fair degree of attention to be convinced that as against any other commonwealth in the United States, we have a greater number of opportunities to maintain prosperity and that we can advance in material wealth in proportion as we seize the advantages which are open to us in every direction. In the larger cities such as Ogden, Provo, Logan and Salt Lake City a genuine jobbing trade is supported. We have wholesale jobbing houses devoted exclusively to dry goods, or clothing, or groceries, hardware, fruits and produce, grain, boots and shoes, machinery and other single lines. Their trade is not confined to this Territory alone, but extends for hundreds of miles into other regions. In Salt Lake City the Mercantile Agencies, Dun's and Bradstreet's have important offices. Reports are made daily to the trade, and hundreds of subscribers maintain this important feature of a commercial center. Not a few of the central cities of the Territory have traders and merchants engaged in gathering together the products of the Territory for export to remote distances. Grain, seeds, hides, wool, live-stock, tallow, furs, skins, eggs, butter, poultry, green fruits and vegetables, dried fruits and such things, usually sent out in carload lots, return a considerable revenue to many of the towns and cities adjacent to the railways. Besides this, those engaged in developing the mineral and other resources of the Territory, ship a great many carloads of stone, marble, onyx, asphaltum, plaster of Paris, fire brick, etc., both East and West. The shipment of ores and bullion, gold, silver and copper is confined principally to the work of the banks and smelters, and this more than all else, brings the ready money into the avenues of trade and finance. Our imports are large,— much too large when we consider the opportunities for manufacture that exist but are neglected in our midst;— but it is not to be supposed that our net imports are measured by the railroad returns, because a large proportion of what we bring in is again sent out into the surrounding country by our jobbers. In a number of the larger cities, some of the retail stores are as fine as any in the West. A statistical investigation made in 1890 showed that there were 1722 stores in Utah, having over twenty million dollars invested. The annual sales of these establishments amounted to over forty-five millions of dollars. There were 7887 employes, and their wages for that year were $4,880,112. It would not be easy to arrive at the aggregate of the commercial and trade transactions of the Territory, but they probably amount to about two hundred millions of dollars annually. The general credit of the merchants and traders of Utah Territory is first class. Failures are comparatively few. There are forty-four banks in Utah, with an aggregate capital of $8,178,758, and deposits estimated at about twice that sum. The developments in this direction may be realized by a comparison with the report for 1879, giving the banks of Utah as eleven in number, with capital of $750,000. During the last four years Salt Lake City has enjoyed the distinction of having a Clearing House. The bank clearings last year were $58,456,129. Salt Lake City has five National banks, eight private and state banks and three savings banks, and it is a matter of local pride and a proof of their financial steadiness that during the panic of 1893, when so many banks failed in all parts of the United States, Salt Lake City kept a clear record, and every one of its banks kept "open house" without even a suspicion of embarrassment. The larger cities of the Territory maintain post-offices of unusual importance. That of Salt Lake City is the only post-office in the interior of the first class. It is one of the best arranged and managed offices in the Union. Its money order business last year was $671,758; 105,000 registered packages were handled, and nearly a million dollars was received in deposits from the subordinate post-offices of Utah, Idaho and Nevada. Its local business for 1893 showed an increase of about thirty per cent. over the previous year. There are many insurance agents located in the principal cities of the Territory, representing fifty companies. Scarcely any of the principal fire and life insurance companies doing business in America are without representation in Utah. Owing to the healthful climate, life insurance companies are active in this field. The sum total of taxable property in the Territory, as the returns by counties to the Territorial auditor for 1893 show, is $115,114,482. Large as this sum appears, it must be remembered that mines, irrigation properties and some industrial plants are exempt from taxation, and not included in the assessment.

Transportation Facilities.—Nearly every year shows some increase in the railway mileage of the Territory, but in 1893, owing to the unpleasantness in national finances, but little development was made, and this consisted of short spurs constructed from the main arteries to stone and other deposits that existed only a few miles distant. Exceptions to this, however, were the completion of a branch of the Rio Grande Western through Sanpete valley at a cost of $250,000, and the construction of the Salt Lake and Los Angeles Railway to Saltair Beach, at a cost of $200,000. The Union Pacific, on its trans-continental course in connection with the Central Pacific, passes through the Territory somewhat north of its center, taking in Ogden on its main line. From this point an important branch strikes southward for several hundred miles, ending at Frisco, in Beaver County, and traversing on its route the more important of the mineral and agricultural districts lying along the western flank of the Wasatch mountains. This line is much more than a feeder for the Union Pacific. It maintains a great local traffic, and furnishes a valuable means of communication between the various counties of the Territory, and gives many of them opportunities for export that they would not otherwise possess. This branch furnishes to the great overland route a large volume of business, both inward and outward, and maintains active operations in the transportation of live stock, merchandise, grain and miscellaneous traffic. The Union Pacific also operates a line running west from Salt Lake City some twenty miles to the famous Garfield Beach, one of the great bathing resorts on the shore of the Great Salt Lake.

Not less important is the splendidly equipped Rio Grande Western Railway, another trans-continental line, which enters the Territory near Grand Junction in the south-eastern part and sweeps to the north-west, to Ogden, where it also connects with the Central Pacific. Along its line are many important shipping points, which supply it with an enormous business in every variety of traffic. It carries the great bulk of the coal and a large proportion of the ores of the Territory. It is a flourishing line, being one of the well-paying railroads of the West, and has a constantly increasing local business, which benefits the road as well as the district through which it runs. It maintains a number of branches or feeders, the longest and most important being that to the Tintic range with its mining interests, and another into the rich agricultural districts of Sanpete and Sevier valleys. Spurs also run to the Pleasant Valley coal mines and to the mining districts of Bingham and Little Cottonwood. The Utah Central is an independent railway line from Salt Lake City to the mines at Park City in Summit County. An important feature of its traffic is derived from the hard sandstone quarries of the Mountain and Metropolitan Stone Companies, near Park City, from which point a very heavy tonnage is handled. The Salt Lake and Los Angeles railroad is another independent line, standard guage, and finely equipped, running from Salt Lake City to the great Saltair Beach bathing resort, a distance of about fourteen miles. The ultimate destination of this road, however, is the Deep Creek mining region in the western part of the Territory, and thence via Southern California to Los Angeles, an extension that will shortly follow with an improved condition in finances. In some of the larger cities of the Territory, notably in Salt Lake City, big railroad companies of the East and West maintain their branch offices, with resident agents. Among the most active are the agencies of the Santa Fe, Colorado Midland, Chicago, Milwaukee, & St. Paul, Missouri Pacific, Chicago & Northwestern, the Burlington and the Denver & Rio Grande. The traffic to be secured by such representation makes the expense thoroughly worth while to these big roads.

Utah looks forward with great hopes to a connection likely to be established with Southern California by the completion of the Nevada Southern, now in actual operation for about 35 miles northward from Blake Station on the Atlantic & Pacific railway and in course of construction through many rich mining districts in Southern Utah to its prospective terminus at Cedar City in the great iron and coal regions of Iron County, from which point connection will then be promptly made with the Southern extensions of the R. G. W. & U. P. lines in central Utah. Another railway projected to bring Utah into close con-

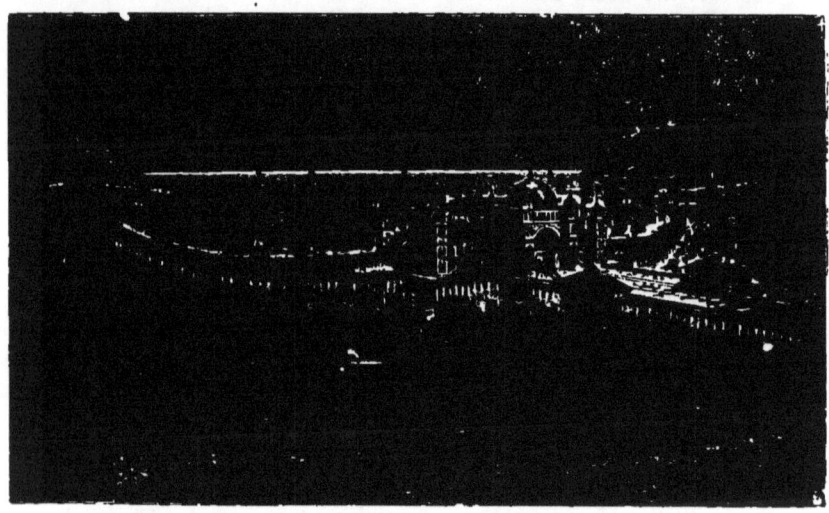

SALTAIR BEACH BATHING RESORT.

nection with Southern California, is the Utah, Nevada and California line, destined to operate between Provo in Utah County, and a point on the Atlantic & Pacific. Still another road in contemplation is the Utah & Los Angeles Air Line, to be built by a New York company. The preliminaries of this organization indicate that a route as direct as possible will be followed, in which case St. George and "Dixie" will be important points on its course.

In Ogden, Provo, and in Salt Lake City, street railways have been in operation for a number of years. Two strong, active companies furnish transit in Salt Lake City and their equipment will compare favorably with that of many of the largest cities of the East.

INDUSTRIES.

The subject of home industries has commanded the attention of the people of Utah from the time of its first settlement. Isolated as it was in the beginning, necessity compelled the production of many articles which other communities import, and drove the people into finding means to manufacture them. It was thus revealed that from the many resources that lie about us a large proportion of the materials used at home could be made here, and in early times the self-supplying faculty of the residents of this Territory was developed under great difficulties, and they learned to do many things in a primitive way that have since been refined upon and expanded until the quality and quantity of the goods manufactured in this Territory are by no means insignificant. . "Home manufacture" has been so long and so steadily a familiar watchword with the people of Utah that there are not many communities in the West that have attempted such various lines of industry. Not all of these have succeeded,' yet we will bear comparison with many older states. There is a genuine determination among the people of Utah to establish and sustain the manufacturing interests of the Territory. We accuse ourselves and each other of a lack of interest in these matters, but this only shows that we are alive to the necessity. The volume of manufactured material produced is a proof of our sincerity in this direction. The leaders of the people in early times told them that they had all the material necessary to make them one of the most prosperous and independent peoples on earth, if they would only make use of the material that nature had placed at their disposal. Repeated efforts under adverse circumstances gave the start to a manufacturing community, and as early as 1850 the industrial products of Utah amounted to $291,220. In 1860 this amount had increased to $900,153. Ten years later, according to the census returns, it was 2,343,019, and in 1890 the returns showed that there were 310 enterprises of this character in operation, turning out a product valued at $5,836,003. The capital invested was $4,405,881. The plants cost $3,215,511, and they used that year, raw material worth $2,137,291. 3274 hands were employed, and the wages paid were $1,597,177. We have good reason to believe these figures to be under statements even for 1890, but were the data of to-day obtainable, a considerable increase would now be shown; but these dry figures must impress every thoughtful reader that the people of Utah engage heartily in the development of their industrial possibilities, and by this means maintain their prosperity and contribute to the well being of the population. In manufactures, as in the other resources dwelt upon in this pamphlet, we must again refer to their almost infinite variety, which sustains our proposition that the opportunities for enterprise in this Territory are multiform almost beyond belief. We do not wish to burden these pages with statistical tables, but will content ourselves with a brief reference to some of the leading articles of manufacture produced within the Territory; but before going into details it is proper to testify to the stimulating effect upon our industries that has been felt through the operations of the Deseret Agricultural and Manufacturing Society of Utah, which for many years has called upon the manufacturers to gather together an exhibition of their products to be set before the people at the annual fairs that have

BEET FIELD, UTAH CO. 39 TONS TO ACRE.

been held in Salt Lake City. Manufacturing and commerce, transforming crude substances into articles of value and beauty, distributing and selling them; these are the indispensable evidences of wealth and prosperity; but manufactures need fostering, and it is proper that the manufacturer should be favored by the community. This has been as well understood and as fully practiced in Utah as in any other part of the West, but during the last few months there has been a drawing together of those engaged in industrial pursuits, and an extensive movement is on foot to lighten the burdens of the manufacturers and to excite the people of the Territory to a fuller appreciation of the importance of their labors.

The Great Copper Plant.—On the outskirts of Salt Lake City there has been almost completed one of the most stupendous industrial enterprises that exists in the Western country. It consists of the largest copper plant of its kind in the world, to be owned and operated by the Salt Lake City Copper Manufacturing Company. It will begin operations within a month or two, and by that time $500,000 will have been spent on the plant alone. It will have a capacity for smelting from 250 to 300 tons of copper per day; the principal source of ore supply being from the Copperopolis group in Juab County, the Copper Mountain in Box Elder County, and the Nancy Hanks group in Nevada. The product of these works will be fine copper in the shape of wire, bars, cakes, sheets or ingots as the market demands, and in the refining department fine gold and silver will be produced. Storage houses have been erected capable of holding 5000 tons of ore, and the heavy handling at the works will be done by electric travellers. Powerful crushers will reduce the ore ready for the blasting furnaces, which latter have a capacity of 150 tons per day; here ores will be reduced or transformed to copper matte. Thence the product will be taken to the converter plant, from which the copper will be delivered 98 per cent. pure. It is then ready for casting into shape for treatment by the electrolitical process. This will be accomplished in a building 364 feet long and 180 feet wide, supplied with five large Elwell dynamos with a capacity for turning out forty tons of fine copper per day. The power for this portion of the plant is derived from a one thousand horse power triple expansion engine, the one which secured the first prize in Machinery Hall at the World's Fair, and was pronounced the finest engine of its kind ever made. It is now being put in place. The process consists of dissolving the copper in an acid solution, from which the electric current deposits it in an absolutely pure condition on sheets of paper. During this process the gold and silver contained in the copper are separately collected, and after undergoing a cleansing process are ready for the mint. The boiler house contains eleven boilers and another triple expansion engine of three hundred horse power supplies the motive power for other portions of the plant. The operations of this concern will not only furnish a ready market for the copper produced in our midst, but other industries will spring up in the manufacture of copper-ware of every description. Salt Lake City contributed a bonus of $100,000 to induce the location of these works within its limits, and this alone should be proof of the willingness of our people to contribute towards the inauguration of legitimate manufacturing institutions.

Woolen Mills.—Woolen mills are in operation in Salt Lake, Utah, Beaver and Washington Counties. The largest and most important of these is the Provo Woolen Mills, whose annual output is $150,000, and which employs 125 hands, consuming 400,000 pounds of Utah wool. A description of this enterprise and of another woolen mill at Springville is to be found under the head of Utah County. A large proportion of the cloth manufactured at Provo is sent to California, Colorado and other states, where it finds favor in competition with the finest mills of the East and West. The Deseret Woolen Mills in Salt Lake City is another extensive establishment, manufacturing fine woolen dress goods, flannels, yarns and a fine grade of white blankets. Sixty persons are employed and about 200,000 pounds

PROVO WOOLEN MILLS.

of Utah wool used annually. A big knitting factory is operated in connection with these works. A great deal of the fine cloth manufactured there and at the Provo mills is used by the merchant tailors of the larger cities, besides big shipments that are sent away. In their splendid wearing qualities as well as in their fine appearance the cassimeres and other suitings turned out by these works are held in high esteem.

The woolen mills located in other parts of the Territory are by no means small, but their product is chiefly consumed in the neighborhood of the factories.

Sugar.—The Lehi Sugar Factory in Utah County is one of the biggest manufacturing institutions that we have. The production last year was 3,877,110 pounds of first quality granulated sugar. A fuller description of this enterprise is included in the statement furnished by Utah County on another page. These works are the largest in America engaged in the manufacture of beet sugar, and they are also the finest and most perfect in their appointments. They are looked upon as a model institution, and are usually visited by those who propose the erection of similar works in other parts of the country.

Soap Works.—Soap making has been carried on in Utah for a great many years, but of late the production has largely increased. Three factories are in operation in Salt Lake and one in Ogden; the output is now 100,000 pounds per month, and the local market at least will shortly be supplied almost entirely with soap of Utah manufacture.

Boots and Shoes.—There are four or five hundred hands employed in Utah in shoe factories, most of them in Salt Lake, but some in Ogden, Logan, Provo, Lehi, Spanish Fork and other country towns. The largest of these concerns are in Salt Lake City; one of them operated by the Zion's Co-operative Mercantile Institution, employing about two hundred hands, and turning out annually nearly $200,000 in manufactured material. This, however, does not represent the possibilities of manufacture in this direction, as it has been computed that the requirements of this Territory alone would give employment to 800 men, producing boots and shoes to the amount of one million dollars.

Clothing.—Besides a very considerable amount of clothing produced by the tailoring establishments throughout the Territory, there is one concern at least that is engaged in the manufacture of clothing on a large scale. The Zion's Co-operative Mercantile Institution at Salt Lake City employs sixty people on overalls alone, having an output valued at $57,000. A great many shirts and other garments are also sold from this and other factories.

SILK CULTURE IN UTAH.

BY MRS. MARGARET A. CAINE.

ONE of the very important resources of the Territory which attracted marked attention at the Columbian Exposition, was the Utah Silk Exhibit at the Woman's Building; and we fully realize that the opportunity given us to exhibit our silk to the world is due to Mrs. Potter Palmer, President of the Board of Lady Managers, whose intelligent sympathy and keen appreciation of the needs of industrial women rendered her the constant champion of this worthy enterprise.

Today the annual importation of unprepared silk alone into the United States amounts to over $35,000,000, and the quality of silk which they procure is such that our manufacturers cannot discover the art of putting a luster on it which will last, or give us a fabric which will in any way compete with the foreign manufactured silk. Apparently there is a lack of knowledge regarding silk in our country. It is supposed that the beauty and luster of the oriental silk is due to some unknown art in manufacturing and dyeing, and that *all silk* is of very nearly the same quality. This is a mistake. There are as many grades of silk as you may expect to find of fruit in an orchard. By thoroughly understanding the nature of the worms, and providing them with proper food, the grades may be controlled by the producer. Yet it is as impracticable to attempt to produce only the best grade of silk as of any agricultural product.

The great fair just over has given us an opportunity to learn something of what has been done in this industry. We find that silk has been produced to a considerable extent in Connecticut, New York, New Jersey, Pennsylvania, Illinois, Kansas, California, Georgia and Florida; in fact in almost every state in the Union, and in most cases by women. No doubt in many parts of our country where the mulberry will grow, a much better quality of silk can be produced than is now being imported; but as the climate has much to do with the quality and luster of the silk, we feel confident that in America, Utah will be the home of the silk worm, for our silk contains the same luster, elasticity and durability as that which can be produced in any country in the world.

This industry in Utah began in the year 1855 or 1856. In the past it has been carried on mostly in the homes of the people, though much has also been done in a public way. Brigham Young, when Governor of Utah, procured a supply of mulberry seed from France, and in a few years fifty acres of mulberry trees were planted in orchards and groves of Salt Lake and Utah Counties. From that time they have been grown in all parts of the Territory, in nearly every town and village, and they have flourished luxuriantly; it is estimated that there are at least two hundred and fifty acres of mulberry trees in Utah at present.

The services of some experienced sericulturists from France and Italy, have been secured to give instructions to the people in raising the worms. Under the direction of Mrs. Dunyon, there were raised in six weeks, seven hundred pounds of cocoons, which at that time were worth $2 00 per pound in France.

In 1876 a Territorial organization was effected, called the Deseret Silk Association, (Mrs. Zina D. H. Young, President) for the purpose of promoting the industry by means of united efforts. Auxiliary associations were formed in several counties in which women were active directors and practical workers. Cocoons were raised in large quantities, but for lack of means manufactories were not permanently established. During one year this association paid to operators $1,500, and the quantity of silk prepared was four hundred pounds. There have been raised in Utah over twenty-eight thousand pounds of cocoons.

Utah silk was exhibited at the Centennial celebration in Philadelphia, and examined by experts who attested to its excellence, and awarded a diploma. Utah cocoons have been placed on the market in San Francisco and Philadelphia, and pronounced of very superior quality. During the failure of silk worms in France, a large quantity of eggs were sent there, which were considered by them to be very good, and for which we received a very high price. This for a time found a market for large quantities of cocoons also.

In the manufactories of the East, little has been done in reeling silk, and as there is no duty on the unprepared silk (while all manufactured silk is imported under a heavy duty) they seem to prefer importing silk in bales. Because of the inexperience of the producers of silk in Utah, our reeled silk could not pass the examination to which it was subjected, therefore could not be disposed of. At one time the manufacturing of silk thread was quite extensively and successfully carried on by Judge Alexander Pyper in Salt Lake City, and for some time the Z. C. M. I. Shoe Factory was supplied with thread, which, it is said, was very much better than any they have ever been able to import. It was also much desired by saddle and harness makers because of its superior strength. This enterprising industry was brought to a sudden end by the death of its promoter, while railway connection with the markets of the east ended the necessity for the mother to make the cloth with which she clothed her family, and the culture of silk was becoming a thing of the past. But we are now being made aware of the fact that with our rapidly increasing population, every resource of the country must be fully developed, and we hope in the near future to establish manufactories and to do the work perfectly.

When the Board of Lady Managers sent an invitation to the women of Utah, desiring them to contribute something to the decoration of the Woman's Building, at the World's Fair, it was decided that nothing would be more representative of the thrift and industry of the Territory and so entirely woman's work as a pair of homemade silk portiers, the design to be the Sego Lily (the floral emblem of Utah) designed and embroidered by our own ladies. The portiers, as a proof of our wise selection, were received with profound surprise, it not having been known that such a quality of silk could be produced in America.

Mrs. Margaret B. Salisbury, National Commissioner from Utah, was asked if Utah could make an exhibit of silk, which might lead to the encouragement of sericulture in the United States, if an appropriation were obtained from Congress. The money being procured the offer was accepted, although the Fair was then open. As no silk had been produced for four years this was no easy task at home, yet we succeeded in collecting a number of silk dresses, silk shawls, scarfs, fringes, hosiery, knitting and sewing silk and twists, a quantity of reeled silk and cocoons, which, with the portiers, made our cases both artistic and interesting. We also engaged a young lady, born and reared in Utah, to reel, and a woman to weave, and procured a primitive loom, reel and twisting wheel, with all attachments, which had been used here in the early days. This exhibit attracted a great deal of attention and in the last catalogue issued, it was prominently mentioned as one of the most interesting exhibits in the Woman's Building, and of especial interest to industrial women. Among those who visited it were many foreigners, experienced in sericulture, who were very much interested. One Frenchman, who was engaged in selling French silks in America, said of one piece of silk in the exhibit "that if we could produce silk of that quality, we had an unknown source of wealth which, if properly manipulated, would be more to us than any amount of gold." Many kindergarten workers took notes of every detail, and thought it would be a wonderful thing to introduce into their work. Women interested in industrial homes were just as anxious to investigate the work, and felt confident, that if taken up in a simple way, would furnish interesting employment for their girls, which might in time bring a very profitable remuneration. We sincerely trust the exhibit will do a great deal of good in the direction for which it is intended, and that we will fully appreciate the benefits which it has brought to us at home. Our silk was examined by a committee of Japanese under the department of manufacture, and awarded a medal and a diploma, and under the department of agriculture by American experts, who also awarded it a medal and a diploma. Besides this the exhibitors obtained a vast amount of valuable information from the Fair and its visitors regarding the methods of raising and preparing silk before unknown to them. In addition to the exhibit made at the Woman's Building, the ladies of Davis County contributed a set of furniture to the Fair for the ladies' reception room in the Utah Building The pieces, seven in all, were upholstered in home-made silk, sage green in color, brocaded with a spray of wild sage, the tone harmonizing with the other furnishings in the room. The upper part of the windows were festooned very artistically with cocoons. We feel that if the women of Utah can receive some assistance and will take hold of this industry, which is so particularly adapted to women, and permanently establish it, it will give labor of a profitable nature to many of our women and be a great benefit to the nation, by keeping at home a vast amount of money. The raising of the worms is a labor which is extremely interesting, and the reeling demands an acute and gentle touch found only in the hands of women. The weaving furnishes a broad field for artistic work in coloring and designing, as well as light labor, and will bring to any industrious woman a profitable remuneration.

As has been stated, there are thousands of mulberry trees already growing, the climate is well adapted to the silk worm; the country is free from disease which is so fatal in damp climates, and with hundreds of women anxious to engage in the industry, things look propitious for the development of an industry which will be a source of considerable wealth and revenue to the territory.

Flouring Mills.—A number of large roller mills are in operation in different parts of the Territory, the principal ones being located in the large cities and in the great grain producing districts of Cache and Sanpete. Their product is not excelled by any flour made in America. With fullest opportunities for selection of wheat for making flour up to the best standard, they usually run all the year round. Some of the mills manufacture oatmeal, cracked wheat, pearl barley, hominy, etc., all of very high quality.

Breweries.—Utah beer has a high reputation wherever it is introduced, and its manufacture is one of the most important industries of Salt Lake City. There are three breweries there, the largest of which makes 20,000 barrels of beer per annum and bottles 600 dozen per day. They are equipped with fine bottling works and ice machines. Considerable export business is done. *Aerated waters* are also manufactured in Ogden, Salt Lake and several other of the larger cities, and this is an industry which is rapidly increasing in importance.

Brick Making.—This is an important industry, carried on largely in Weber, Salt Lake and Utah Counties, and on a lesser scale in many other counties of the Territory. The quality of brick manufactured in Beaver County is exceedingly fine. There are twelve yards in the neighborhood of Salt Lake City, producing about thirty million brick annually, and in Ogden several yards have a large business. A great improvement has taken place in the manufacture of brick in Utah during the last two years. A splendid collection of our work was shown at the World's Fair and secured a prize. Fire brick is also manufactured here of a quality that stands the highest test, and commands a good price.

The *charcoal* industry furnishes employment to a great many men, the product being chiefly consumed in the smelting operations near Salt Lake City. Emery and Utah Counties lead in this industry.

The manufacture of *Portland cement* is one of the big industries about to be inaugurated. A company has invested $100,000 in this branch of manufacture at Salt Lake City, with a capacity of 200 barrels of cement per day. They will also manufacture tile brick, terra cotta and other cement products. There is no question that its output will be exceptionally fine in quality, stopping the heavy importations of the past few years and probably securing a large export trade.

The *Machine Shops* and *Foundries* of the larger cities represent a considerable investment and turn out several hundred thousand dollars worth of manufactured iron and machinery annually. A great deal of their work consists of repairs, but several of the principal conerns are well equipped with improved appliances and can manufacture big engines complete.

Among the other industrial concerns operating in various cities of the Territory, are many saw mills, lath and planing mills, stone quarries, lime kilns, potteries, tanneries, factories for polishing gems, knitting factories, canneries and concerns which manufacture brooms, brushes, vehicles, ice, confectionery, mattresses, crackers, show cases, vinegar, plaster of Paris, steam boilers, harness, cut stone, paper boxes, rubber stamps, coffins, mosaic tiles, picture frames, upholstery, chemicals, fur goods, gloves, pickles, iron fencing, etc. The James-Spencer-Bateman Company of Salt Lake City manufacture lead pipe, bar lead and solder of fine quality, supplying Utah entirely, and ship some out of the Territory. Their product for 1893 was 268,083 pounds of lead pipe, valued at nearly $20,000. The lead used was refined by the Germania Lead Works in Salt Lake County.

Notwithstanding the great variety of manufacturing concerns which we have described, opportunities are open for still others to be inaugurated, which can undoubtedly be made to pay good returns on the amount invested. Among them have been suggested cotton mills, a carpet factory, paper mills to replace those which recently burned in Salt Lake County; works for the manufacture of agricultural implements, white lead, gunpowder, whiting, iron pipe, sewer-pipe, window glass and bottles, soda-ash, putty, starch, candles, paints, etc. Application has been made by the delegate of Utah for the establishment of a branch mint at Salt Lake City for the coinage of silver.

UTAH MANUFACTURERS BUREAU.

A movement has recently been commenced by the Manufacturers Bureau of the Salt Lake Chamber of Commerce which will undoubtedly encourage and support home industries in this Territory. A number of vigorous citizens have leagued together to arouse all the people of the inter-mountain region to support such enterprises, and by public appeals they have excited a great deal of renewed interest in the subject. Each householder is being supplied with a list of the articles manufactured, and every consumer is being urged to make it his individual duty to forward the movement. The stimulating effect of this crusade is being felt in every direction. The citizens generally are calling for goods made at home and find that they are superior in quality and worthy of all the endorsement they can give. New branches of industry are being considered, while great encouragement is being given to those that are already engaged in industrial pursuits. An era of prosperity seems to have overtaken those engaged in home manufacture, and the war cry is now "Western made goods for Western people." The attitude of the East on the silver and lead questions has awakened a spirit of independence among the people of this Territory, who find that they can produce a vast amount of material that has heretofore been imported. There seems a unanimous determination to test this point to the utmost, and to their delight they see that millions of dollars may be kept in their hands by manufacturing many of the leading articles which they have been bringing in from afar. The crude materials exist on every side in abundance, labor is plentiful and willing, Colorado and other surrounding States are in thorough accord with the movement, and the industrial developments among the western mountains in the near future promise to be of such a magnitude that they will put a new phase on the relations between the East and the West.

RANCH AND RANGE INTERESTS.

If our climate is too dry for the luxuriant growth of grasses in the valleys throughout the summer, the conformation of our Territory is such that it fully offsets to the stock-raiser whatever drawbacks may be laid to the want of summer rains. As the feed begins to give out on the lower benches in the spring, the snow line is receding on the foot hills, and stock is pastured at higher altitudes as the season advances, until in the midsummer they graze among the grassy valleys of the mountains and on the cool high plateaus. When winter approaches they gradually retire again, and by the time of general snow-fall are roaming over low wide ranges where they cannot exist in summer for heat and want of water. This changing life brings them health and hardihood. They have a "summer out" every year, and are thus developed into the sturdiest races of America. The ranges of one season are held in reserve at another. During the summer, on the millions of acres of the interior basins, too dry for summer ranges, the native bunch grass is maturing and cures, standing, ready for the immense flocks and herds which will winter there. In these regions the snow-fall is light, enough to furnish water for the stock, but not to bury the dry fattening bunch grass, famous for its nutritive qualities. Such, in round terms, is the manner of raising cattle, horses and sheep in Utah, and the quintupling of these interests in the last six years is sufficient proof of its excellence. Add to these products the wool, hides, honey, butter and cheese, dried fruits, wine and cider, vinegar and sorghum, hogs and other products of ranch and range, and the amount which this, with all our resources, contributes to the revenue of the Territory is extremely important. In 1890 it was estimated that the value of the possessions of ranch and range amounted to $12,616,697.25; but the Territorial statistician himself expressed a belief that the unreported possessions bent upon escaping the assessor's valuation were fully one-half as much again.

The *Cattle* interests of Utah are receiving great attention, and a marked improvement in the breeds has been noticed during the past few years. Durham, Hereford, and Holstein are in principal favor. Exports are made nearly every year, but by far the greater portion of our beef is consumed at home. More than one excellent judge has said that there is no place where they eat such good juicy beef as in Utah.

Sheep.—There are probably 3,000,000 sheep in Utah, valued at nearly $6,000,000. The wool-clip approximates 12,000,000 pounds per annum. A sudden grading up has taken place among large holders in the past three years, from the original Mexican stock to Cotswold and Spanish and French merinos. This has given good results in the fineness of wool. The sheep industry is pretty well distributed throughout the Territory, Sanpete County taking the lead.

Utah range *horses* are better animals for their weight and size than any others in America. They have been crossed for the past few years from the native to the Hambletonian and other leading breeds of America. Utah is now therefore an important horse market with a wide reputation for the excellence of her stock, for light driving and saddle horses. They excel in fleetness, wind and in endurance, and for several years past work and farm horses, fancy roadsters, fine carriage and heavy freight horses have been raised. The mountain qualities of strong feet and lungs remain with the horse after he has been exported, and for this reason Utah horses are in steady demand. Cache valley in particular has produced some magnificent animals, and more than one famous trotter has been born and reared in this Territory to make a name for himself among the fast horses of the East.

Among other articles of export which bring us revenue are sheep pelts, hides, flint deer-hides and buckskin, furs, such as muskrat, wolf, beaver, lynx, fox, bear, badger, mink, wild-cat and others are also shipped in considerable quantities. The output of honey alone approaches $100,000. The production of butter is not less than $500,000; beeswax, cheese for home consumption, eggs and poultry also contribute revenue to the husbandman. Garfield County is the greatest producer of cheese, although Cache Valley people give it considerable attention. Fifty thousand gallons of wine, worth as many dollars, are annually produced in the southern portion of the Territory; cider in many places; dried fruits, especially peaches, form a staple article of trade, a number of carloads being annually exported. They become very dry and are not so handsome as some, but for flavor and real value they command the highest price in Chicago and other Eastern cities. These figures are given at the risk of rendering our pages tedious, but they cannot fail to be convincing. We feel that the mere assertion that such a wonderful variety of products issue from our ranges, farms and farm-yards might well give rise to doubts as to the truth of such statements; but every claim made in this work is based upon indisputable facts, susceptible of proof; and if these things can be truthfully said, they should not be withheld from the reader who desires to inform himself regarding the sources of prosperity that exist in this wonderful Territory. But that they might become tiresome far greater details are at hand and might be given.

SOCIAL AFFAIRS AND AMUSEMENTS.

For forty years, the peculiar social conditions that existed in Utah gave it a certain renown that made it of interest to tourists and travelers, but this sort of regard was not calculated to forward our material affairs. The attention of visitors was so taken up with the social and religious aspects of the people living here that enquiry was seldom made as to the resources of the Territory. Although there never was a more peaceful people, and acts of violence were very rare, dissentions and turbulent arguments were plenty and party prejudice was intense. This lased until five or six years ago, and had much to do with the benighted conditions of the people of the country as to our real opportunities for material advancement. When a visitor of any judgment comes to a new country he generally enquires as to its resources; he wants to know about the agriculture of the country, its manufactures, mineral and other advantages; but up to a few years ago, every visitor wanted to have a Mormon pointed out to him, wanted to know how many wives every man had whom he met, wanted to see the Mormon churches, and wanted, above all, to do a little missionary work of a religious character; but he rarely, very rarely, thought to enquire why our climate was the very best under the sun, why we could and did produce the greatest crops known to agriculture, why we led the whole mountain country in all the refining arts of peace, or what truth there was in the report that we had a greater number of sources of prosperity than any other state in the Union. Today, however, such a visitor would be looked upon as a back-number,— the old-time enquiries would stamp him as one who had been stranded on the shores of time, and had let the world run past him. In a most courteous way he would be given to understand that we have forgotten how to answer such questions. The practices to which they refer have been relegated to ancient history, and we have other things to tell him which pertain to the present and the future,—facts more wonderful and more essential, such, for instance, as those which fill the pages of this book,

and by the mere telling of our resources of land and air and sea, his curiosity regarding the history of the past is effaced and a new interest is aroused. Then he begins to understand Utah as it is to-day, and realizes that the people of Utah are fraternal, progressive and well abreast of the American tide of advancement; that in each town and hamlet, there is a marked degree of ambition toward refinement and intellectual development,—for there is not a settlement without its literary and improvement association,—and in music, painting, oratory, social culture, and in general educational matters, the people occupy the front ranks with any Western commonwealth. Among the other good things that Utah has to say for herself, these are not to be overlooked, for, notwithstanding the allurements of better health and prosperity, many excellent people accustomed to social advantages and refinements, have hesitated to make a home in the West, because they fear to lose the opportunities of intellectual culture for themselves and their children. There need be no such fear. In the larger cities of Utah, there are art associations, literary clubs, a university club, press club, lodges of all the leading Masonic, Odd-Fellow, and other secret aid societies, fine churches of nearly every religious denomination, dramatic associations, public libraries, and similar institutions that go to make up a cultured environment. At a recent exhibition of paintings by the Society of Utah Artists, a great many original paintings of much merit proved that in this branch of art we have developed further than any other state between Illinois and California. Several Utah artists were represented at the World's Fair, and some of their works were purchased by the City of Chicago for the permanent exhibition. In music, Utah has accomplished so much that it deserves to be treated in a separate article, and the following has been compiled for this work by Dr. Ellen B. Ferguson, of Salt Lake City:

HISTORY OF MUSIC IN UTAH.

The sovereignty of the realm of music in America had long been divided among the older cities of the republic, when in 1893, Utah, the young giant of the Rocky Mountains, entered the arena to contest for the World's Fair prizes, and sent to Chicago a picked choir of 250 voices to compete with the artistic and famed choral organizations of the Old and New World, for the crowning honors of the World's Fair Eisteddfod. Much admiration was expressed for the nerve and pluck of this ambitious but hitherto undistinguished competitor, but this was changed to astonishment and wonder, when the Utah choir stepped triumphantly to the second place among the successful contestants, and almost snatched from the brows of the Cymric bards the laurels of their forefathers. The following brief history of music in Utah will show the gradual development of the divine art in this Territory, and the steps that led to the attainment of the present elevated standard of musical taste and culture in the community, and rendered possible the magnificent achievements of the Salt Lake choir.

In the growth of civilization, and the unfolding of social development, music and her twin sister poetry take precedence of all the arts, and present an

SOCIAL AFFAIRS AND AMUSEMENTS. 51

unmistakable index to national character. The pioneer settlers who crossed the Rocky Mountains to make homes in the valley of the Great Salt Lake, were certain in the early stage of their peculiar civilization to manifest the genius of music, and the hosts of Israel beguiled many an hour of their weary march across the continent by singing the songs of Zion.

The first musical organization formed in Utah was a brass band composed of fifteen musicians, under the leadership of Captain William Pitt, which commenced its labors in 1850, and for several years furnished the music on every anniversary and local celebration and assisted, the first dramatic association in its representations. In 1851 Dominico Ballo, an Italian, highly endowed with the musical genius of his race, came to Salt Lake City and electrified the people with his performances on the clarionet, on which instrument he was unrivaled, both in tone, style and execution. Soon after his arrival he organized "Ballo's Band" of twenty instruments, viz., seven B flat clarionets, one E flat, played by himself; two piccolos, two first cornets, two second cornets, one ophicleide, three bass horns, one tenor, trombone, and drums. This combination created great excitement on its first appearance, and continued to gain power and prestige by its skillful rendition of some of the most difficult compositions of the day. Ballo was a fine composer, though but few of his works survive and his name will always be held in reverence as the most cultured of the musical pioneers of Utah.

In 1853 David O. Calder, the pioneer class teacher of vocal music came to Salt Lake City, and settled over Jordan where he taught the first singing school in the Territory. In 1861 he organized two classes of two hundred members each, for instruction in the Curwen tonic sol-fa method, which was the first introduction of the system in America. He compiled, arranged and printed all the class books he used. In 1862 Mr. Calder organized the Deseret Musical Association, composed of two hundred picked singers from the different classes under his tuition This society gave several concerts in the theater and Tabernacle with marked success, and during its existence stimulated musical culture in the community.

In 1862 Professor Charles J. Thomas, who had for years been associated with some of the principal theater orchestras in London, came to Salt Lake City and at once took charge of the orchestra in the new Salt Lake Theater, then just opened, and under his leadership it maintained for several years a high standard of excellence. As conductor of the Tabernacle Choir, Professor Thomas did some creditable work, and he long held a ruling musical position.

Professor John Tullidge also deserves mention at this time as a fine tenor singer and composer, and his name will be remembered as long as his anthem, "How beautiful upon the mountains," delights the ears of a Salt Lake audience.

The man who did most for the early musical progress of Salt Lake City and the establishment of the legitimate profession, is undoubtedly Professor George Careless. Born in London, and trained with some of the best instrumentalists of the day, under the batons of such masters as Sir Michael Costa, Sir Jules Benedict and other famous conductors, Mr. Careless brought to Salt Lake City, in 1865, such musical genius, brilliant execution and talent for leadership, as produced a complete revolution in musical circles, and created quite a furore of enthusiasm among the music loving people of the community. During the earlier years that he waved the baton over the theater orchestra, he produced a number of musical plays, including Macbeth, The Brigand, Aladdin and Cinderella—for the two latter he composed all the music, consisting of solos, duets, choruses and dramatic interludes. During this engagement he conducted the first opera ever given in Utah, "The Grand Duchess," by the Howson troupe.

In 1875 the great musical event of the city was the performance of the oratorio of the Messiah by the Philharmonic Society, under the training and leadership of Professor Careless, with over two hundred singers and a full orchestra. The performance was a great musical triumph, and was pronounced by the critics of the day a presentation far superior both in its vocal and orchestral merit, to one given of the same oratorio in San Francisco, with Madame Anna Bishop and other vocal celebrities in the principal parts. In the instrumentation, the first violins and the cornet obligato, by Mr. Mark Croxall, were particularly fine, while among the vocalists, the palm of excellence belonged without any question to Mrs. Careless, the wife of Professor Careless, whose rendition of the aria, "I know that my Redeemer liveth," was simply perfection. Her pure, sweet, bell-like tones, and exquisite delivery, intense with feeling, rose almost in this selection to the exalted pitch of epic song. The fact that this oratorio could be executed in such perfection by a local association, and call out a cultured audience fully capable of appreciating such music, proves that Salt Lake City even then was one of the great musical centers of the world, a reputation that her subsequent history proudly maintains. Professor Careless also conducted the Parepa Rosa concerts in 1868, the Ann i Bishop concert in the Tabernacle, and the grand Wilhelmj concerts in the Theater in 1880, and received from that great virtuoso the highest praise and many marks of personal esteem.

In 1879 Professor Careless gave Sullivan's opera of "Pinafore," and later "The Mikado," both brilliant successes, and rendered exclusively by home talent, and in 1885 he organized the largest local orchestra ever brought together in this city, consisting of forty-five members. During his partnership in the musical business with Mr. D. O. Calder, the firm imported a large number of pianos, organs, brass and string instruments of all kinds, and published the "Salt Lake Musical Times," the first musical publication issued west of Chicago. For fourteen years Professor Careless was the trainer and conductor of the Tabernacle Choir, and by his faithful and unwearied labors laid the foundation of that artistic excellence which rendered its recent brilliant success possible. To Mrs. Careless, who was for several years the leading soprano of the choir, belongs by right of her rare genius the highest niche of fame among our musical stars. With a voice of phenomenal purity and resonance, united with the most perfect control and culture, she so educated Salt Lake City audiences to quality and sublimity in music that only a Patti could sing here without being adversely compared with her.

The musical history of Salt Lake City would be incomplete without prominent mention of the grand organ in the Tabernacle. When it was commenced in 1866, all the material necessary for building it had to be hauled across the plains and over the Rocky Mountains in wagons. It shows how deeply the love of music was rooted in the hearts of the early settlers in Utah, when in the face of such almost insuperable obstacles, they planned and successfully carried to completion the erection of such a magnificent instrument, at that time the second largest in the world. The architect and designer of this great organ was Mr. Joseph Ridges, who worked on it for many years, but to Mr. Johnson, belongs the credit of bringing it to its present finished perfection. It has four manuals and pedals, fifty-seven stops, and 2,648 pipes, supplied with wind by three large bellows, operated by two hydraulic motors. In its completed form, situated in one of the most perfect acoustic buildings in the world, it is justly an object of pride to our city, and the one grand admiration of strangers.

When Professor Careless resigned the leadership of the Philharmonic Society, Professor Radcliffe came to the city and took the vacant position, and a year later gave the "Creation" in the theater with marked success. Professor Radcliffe is a great organist, and his recitals given on the Tabernacle organ prove his complete mastership of that noble instrument, and have won for him an enviable reputation through all the Rocky Mountain region.

In 1878, in order to meet the growing demand for a more advanced musical education, the Utah Conservatory of music was opened in Salt Lake City, with Dr. Ellen B. Ferguson as director. This institution, devoted to the study of music in all its branches, included systematic courses for the voice and all instruments in common use, with instruction in musical theory, notation, tone, reading and elocution, and was for several years the leading school of music in the Territory; many of its pupils are among our best amateur musicians and vocalists today. Among our local musicians also may be mentioned Professor Joseph J. Daynes, pupil of G. W. Morgan of New York, who has presided at the Tabernacle organ at the choir services since 1867, Professor Beesley, and Professor Orson Pratt, both able teachers of the piano, harmony and counterpoint.

Among our noted violin soloists, Mr. Willard Weihe stands in the front rank. A protege of Ole Bull, for whom he played at the early age of ten years, he has by force of his genius and perseverance worked himself up to the highest position, and under the tuition of the celebrated Vieuxtemps developed a marvelous technique that has rarely been equalled except by a virtuoso. His exquisite rendition of the works of the great masters is at once an inspiration and an artist's dream.

In 1881, Professor H. S. Krouse came to Salt Lake City, and at once established himself as a first-class pianist and teacher, and during his residence here has steadily risen in the appreciation of all lovers of classical music, until he now stands at the head of his profession with a reputation second to none as a teacher of the piano and higher techniques. He excels as a conductor of opera and concert, and his representation of Fatinitza was a brilliant and artistic performance. In this opera Miss Jennie Hawley (now Mrs. H. C. Woodrow), a pupil of Professor Krouse took the title role, in which her exquisite contralto voice was heard to good advantage. In setting before his pupils a high standard of musical taste and culture, and encouraging the study of the works of the most eminent composers, Professor Krouse has done more for the advancement of classical and high art music than any one else in the community, and many of his pupils have become creditable teachers; among whom special mention must be made of Mr. Joseph McIntyre, at present an able and successful teacher in Oneida, N. Y. The annual recitals given by Professor Krouse's pupils are classical entertainments of undoubted merit. The programme for the coming recital includes concertos by Henselt, Chopin and Mendelssohn, with orchestral accompaniment on second piano, also compositions by Liszt, Liebling, Beethoven, Rubenstein, Gottschalk and Wieniawski, rendered by a number of his advanced pupils, who give promise of still greater proficiency in the near future.

A long list of performers on piano, organ, violin and other instruments might be given, which together with a number of vocalists of unusual excellence, justify the claim that we are in Utah a music loving and appreciative people, and that no territory and but few states can equal us in the progress made in the divine art. Especially in this the truth with regard to choral music. Salt Lake leads with the largest church choir in the world, viz , the Tabernacle Choir with six hundred members enrolled The Choral Society with three hundred members; thirty choirs belonging to the various churches in the city, averaging at least twenty voices each, making a grand total of fifteen hundred choir singers in this city alone. Add to these the two hundred and fifty choirs in the various towns and settlements, together with all the Sunday school choristers in the territory, and Utah may well claim to be the land of music, song and sunshine.

To Prof. Evan Stephens, a practical musician and composer of considerable native genius, as well as professional training, is due the success of the general movement in class teaching in the Sunday Schools in the Territory. Possessed of rare personal magnetism, a born musical leader, with perfect choral control, he sways the hundreds of children on the stage with a few simple movements of his baton, maintaining a perfect tempo with the most delicate variations of forte and piano. The concert of National Songs given in the Tabernacle on February 22nd, 1893, by twelve hundred children under fifteen years of age, was one of his most unique efforts, and was repeated seven times to large and enthusiastic audiences. Its success demonstrated the possibility of a high standard of musical training for children, thus educating a generation of musicians who will in future years maintain Utah's musical supremacy in the Rocky Mountains. The greatest achievement of Professor Stephens' career has been the training and successful competition of two hundred and fifty members of the Tabernacle Choir at the World's Fair Eisteddfod. The three competitive choruses were "Worthy is the Lamb" (Messiah), "Blessed are the Men" (Elijah), and "Now the Impetuous Torrents Rise" (David and Saul), and these had been practised for many months by the trained choirs who entered the contest for the World's Fair prizes. The Utah choir, who had less than three months for preparation, sang the numbers without copies, and carried off the second prize of $1,000.00, and in the opinion of many who heard them were entitled to the first honors. The journey of the choir to and from Chicago was a perfect ovation. Performances were given in six of the principal cities en route, and the greatest enthusiasm was manifested by all the people who attended their concerts, while the press was unstinted in praise of their efforts. Utah's triumph in Chicago is only the stimulus to greater endeavor, and the pledge of more brilliant successes in the future. Proud as we may justly be of our past musical achievements and present standing, our future possibilities are far more glorious, and under the leadership of such artists as Krouse, Careless, Stephens, Radcliffe and Weihe, Utah is destined to become world-famed for her unequalled musical excellence and progress.

The scenic attractions of Utah are of world-wide fame. The noble scenery of a thousand canyons and valleys, with their snowy peaks, forests, cliffs, cascades and waterfalls,—the Great Salt Lake, the Grand Canyons of the Colorado, the wild gorges of Southern Utah, and the varied landscapes of the great Uintah and Wasatch ranges have inspired artists, poets and travelers since the earliest days.

An element of great beauty in our mountain scenery is the great number of small fresh water lakes that exist among the upper mountains. They are usually of glacial origin, clear and deep, and lie half hidden among the pine forests which skirt the bases of the high rocky peaks. Near each of the large cities of the territory there are splendid canyons from which the water flows to supply the city. Ogden has two such streams, so has Logan, and along the west flank of the Wasatch Mountains there are scores, each issuing from its separate gorge, and to follow any one of these from its source to its final destination is to traverse a course beset with wild and silvan beauty from one end to the other. But perhaps the most striking scenic charm of the Territory is that the fields and farms, with their pastoral and home-like interest, lie sheltered at the feet of great snowy ranges, the green and fruitful pastures sweeping across the valleys to the rocks at the mountain base, orchards and vineyards being often within a mile or two of immense snow beds and pine forests.

There are many wonderful scenes in Southern Utah, among the approaches to the Colorado river and along its tributaries. The wierd gorges that break into the Rio Virgin river are among the greatest of the scenic wonders of the intermountain west.

THE COUNTIES OF UTAH.

Reference to the annexed diagram will make it easy to understand the relative situation of each county in the Territory without a map. In the following pages, they are described in their alphabetical order. At one time, they might consistently have been grouped into the Northern, Central and Southern Counties, because of their separate interests, but the developments and railway extensions of recent years have drawn them all together into one compact whole, so that the affairs of each county are becoming, year by year, more closely identified with those of all the others. There is not a county in the Territory that is without important mining as well as agricultural interests; each has gold, silver, copper and lead mines, and nearly all have coal, iron and other valuable minerals within their lines; every one has its farms and ranges, and many have well defined industrial possibilities. The residents of the whole Territory can see great cause for hope in future developments, and, together, the counties constitute a union of related interests more diversified than those of any other country of the same area that can be named.

The data from which the following descriptive articles are compiled has been gathered from reliable sources, and in many instances the matter has been submitted by representatives especially appointed for the purpose by the County Courts. Great care has been exercised to make the reports accurate and impartial.

BEAVER COUNTY.

BEAVER COUNTY is situated towards the south-west portion of the Territory, extending from the Beaver range of mountains to the Nevada line. The western portion lacks moisture, but the eastern half is well watered and most fruitful. The Wasatch mountains at this point are magnificent and lofty, supplying Beaver River with numerous tributaries, and securing facilities for irrigation to a large farming population. The average altitude of the agricultural land is about six thousand feet. Alfalfa and small grains are the principal crops, but in some localities there are a few orchards. About two thousand acres are in wheat, which has an average yield of eighteen bushels; the rest being in corn, barley, lucern, hay, potatoes, etc. 323,000 acres of land have been surveyed in Beaver County. It has a great variety of mineral resources and contains several mining districts. Its capital, Beaver City, is one of the principal cities of the south; other towns in the county are Greenville, Adamsville and Milford. The town of Frisco has proven one of the productive mining camps of Utah. Besides the silver and lead producing mines of Beaver County there have been discovered, though but little developed, a number of material resources that may yet be made to sustain an industrial population. Pure silica sand, suitable for glass making, is one thing; another is a really beautiful quality of white marble found near Frisco. From this deposit blocks of any desired size can be quarried at a low cost. It is located adjacent to the Union Pacific system. The population of Beaver County is 3,550, the assessed valuation being $1,220,900.

BOX ELDER COUNTY.

BY A. H. SNOW.

BOX ELDER COUNTY, situated in the northwestern part of Utah, has a population of 8,000. It has under cultivation a little upwards of 30,000 acres, 12,000 of which are irrigated. Here every cereal known to western commerce is successfully grown, the yields being large, many irrigated farms producing fifty bushels of grain and eight tons of alfalfa to the acre. In 1890, when the last official returns were received, this county stood first in the matter of average yield of oats, producing fifty bushels to the acre.

Box Elder has greater inducements for new settlers than any other county in the territory. The great Bear River Canal has been completed at an expense of over two million dollars, and is one of the largest irrigating canals in the United States. Commencing in the great Bear River Canyon and running through the Bear River Valley, the canal extends some 150 miles through as fine a tract of agricultural land as can be found in America. The country would undoubtedly have been settled years ago had it not been for the enormous expense of establishing such a gigantic irrigating scheme. The land adjoins the famous fruit-raising cities of Brigham City, Deweyville, Willard and Honeyville, on the line of the Union Pacific Railway. Brigham City alone shipped on an average, for 1893, eight hundred boxes of fruit per day during the fruit season.

The Bear River Valley covers 150,000 acres of the choicest lands in Utah, proper irrigation for which is now assured. Large crops may thus be depended upon yearly, instead of once in two or three years, as in States where the farmer is compelled to depend upon rain. The water supply from the great Bear River is unlimited. The company controls the water and the farmer is thus assured of an adequate supply of the same at all times. The land is adapted to raising all kinds of fruits, especially peaches, apricots, cherries, plums, strawberries, raspberries and prunes, while wheat, oats, barley and all kinds of roots and garden truck grow splendidly.

On this tract the average crops are as follows:—wheat, 40 bushels to the acre; alfalfa, 5 to 6 tons per acre; potatoes, 2 to 300 bushels to the acre; oats, 75 bushels to the acre, with other crops in proportion.

The company owns 50,000 acres of land, and to encourage settlers they will sell the land and a permanent water right at a reasonable figure and on easy terms. In a recent interview, Mr. W. H. Rowe, who now has charge of the company's affairs, said:

"Just as soon as the season opens 20,000 forest and fruit trees will be planted in the valley, and we will also put in 5,000 acres of lucern and 1,000 acres of grain. The hay will be used as feed for beef, cattle, sheep and hogs, and it will then be unnecessary for the Utah stock growers to send their stock to Nebraska to be fed for market. It is estimated that 25,000 tons of hay at least will be raised on the 5,000 acres of land and this amount of hay will feed a large number of cattle, sheep and hogs. The settlers under the canal have already put in 3,000 acres of winter wheat and more will be put in when spring opens."

Considerable attention is also paid to small farming, dairying, cattle and sheep raising. The latter industry is of special importance, and the sale of wool and mutton is one of the greatest sources of revenue in the county. The western portion of the county is especially adapted for grazing of sheep in the winter, and at this time it is estimated that not less than 100,000 sheep are wintering there.

Brigham City, the county seat of Box Elder County, has a population of 3,000, and is celebrated for its production of large quantities of peaches, strawberries and like fruit, the flavor and quality of which are not surpassed anywhere. The ground seems well adapted for fruit, being of a warm, sandy loam. One Brigham City gardener cleared $475.00 in one season from three-quarters of an acre of strawberries.

Box Elder's mines have not yet a world-wide reputation, but three or four now in course of development are worthy of mention. The Garfield group of mines, owned by the Consolidated Mining & Smelting Co., have been worked for several years and are now beginning to yield valuable returns to the owners. The ore near the surface assays as follows: lead fifty-five per cent; silver five and half ounces; gold $15. to the ton. This would be worth $51.85 per ton. This property is more a gold and lead mine than a silver-lead, which is much in its favor considering the present state of the silver question. The group is situated four miles north of Brigham City and is considered by its owners as a second Ontario.

In the western part of the county a very valuable ledge of mica from three to four miles in length has recently been discovered, which bids fair to cheapen, that expensive commodity in the near future.

Messrs. Toombs and Hickman, says the Brigham City *Bugler*, have been quietly developing a valuable onyx quarry situated on Promontory, twelve miles south of the station on the S. P. Ry. in Box Elder County by that name. They have taken out some beautiful samples, varying from very dark to white. Fine specimens of marble are also found in the vicinity. Representatives of an eastern company have lately been out and inspected the place and they are so well satisfied with the value of the discovery that they have organized a company called the Western Onyx & Marble Co., at Eau Clere, Wis., where they will erect a new plant purposely to work the precious stones from this place. Mr. Toombs says that they expect to put eight or nine men to work on the quarries some time in February. This find may mean thousands for our county.

The assessed valuation of property for the County for 1893 is as follows:

Real Estate. $1,429,627. 00
Improvements including Railway and Telegraph. . . . 2,220,344. 00
Horses, sheep, mules, etc., etc. 625,258. 00

Total . . . $4,275 229. 00

The territorial and school tax for 1893 is $21,000.

CACHE COUNTY.

The fruitful character of Cache County will be realized by a comparison with other portions of the Territory. The county consists of one magnificent valley bordered by high mountains, which are well timbered, and are snow-clad throughout the greater part of the year. From the canyons of these mountains flow generous streams, which give to the whole valley an abundance of water, so that the people are thrifty and well-to-do. Every few miles there is a pleasant town or village, with a few stores and some industrial concerns; but the capital city, Logan, has real commercial importance and is the metropolis of the northern part of the Territory. The general aspect of the county is alpine-pastoral, and excites the admiration of all who love beautiful scenery. Across this broad and beautiful valley there are a quarter of a million acres under cultivation. There is very little land unoccupied, although probably fifty thousand acres more might be cultivated. Six bounteous streams cross the county from east to west, while hundreds of natural springs rise in all parts of the valley. Several hundred flowing wells add to the water supply for market gardening. Wheat, rye, oats, corn and potatoes, can be raised in this county without irrigation, with better results than in any other part of Utah. Seepage has done much to increase the cultivable area, irrigation on the bench lands having rendered the lower lands moist. Wheat easily yields fifty bushels to the acre, and the hay crop is astonishingly great, while alfalfa flourishes luxuriantly. Potatoes and other vegetables yield large crops and are not to be excelled in quality by any in the United States. Fruits, including apples, pears, plums, grapes, strawberries, raspberries, etc., are raised in all parts with profit, and with very little care. Considering the fruitfulness of the soil, cultivated land is to be purchased very reasonably—usually not over $50 per acre. Wheat generally brings 90 cents per bushel; timothy hay about $5.00, and alfalfa $4.00 per ton. The winters are rigorous, and the summers are delightful. Severe winds are unknown. Altogether Cache County is a most attractive district, the climate being superb and the scenery on every side full of beauty. The neighboring canyons are as grand as any in the Territory, and mountain streams afford excellent trout fishing. A number of natural gas wells have been recently secured at a slight cost, and these afford heat and light to the owners. They have been accidentally discovered while driving for water, and the average cost has been less than $100 each.

The county has a population of over 20,000, two semi-weekly newspapers, two banks, eight patent roller flour mills, two electric light plants, and several well-equipped creameries and cheese factories, distributed among seventeen cities and towns, with populations of 500 to 6,000. Large mercantile interests, wholesale and retail, are thriving, and the bulk of the population, following the occupations of the farmer, the cattle, horse and sheep raiser, have become comparatively wealthy from the natural resources about them. Cache County has been justly called "the granary of Utah," and yet there is abundant room for a population of 100,000, and land enough, if properly divided and carefully tilled, for all. Cache Valley horses have a fame throughout a large adjacent country, and her butter and cheese find ready sale as the *best*.

The unused facilities for manufacturing enterprises invite capital, and the water power of Logan River alone offers returns for investment that capital will quickly appreciate, and make use of as soon as known.

The people are intelligent, tolerant and progressive, and it need not be said that a people who would put $600,000.00 into a magnificent Temple, which overlooks the City of Logan, are moral, temperate and industrious.

To home seekers, to investors, to invalids, we say come and live among us.

The altitude of our capital city, Logan, is 4,400 feet, and the mean temperature for 1892 was 51.27, and the death rate is the lowest in Utah.

EDUCATIONAL INTERESTS.

Logan City is the site of the Agricultural College of Utah, which while established as late as 1888, has made stupendous strides and now stands without a rival for excellence, equipment, efficiency and location in the arid region. With an annual national endowment of $40,000.00 for experimental work and scientific research, and an annual appropriation from the state, its future will be a great one and its benefits infinite. Located upon the east slope of Cache

UTAH AGRICULTURAL COLLEGE, LOGAN

Valley and overlooking the beautiful "city of schools," with 110 acres of land improved and alive with vegetation for college experiments, with buildings and apparatus worth $200,000.00, it is the pride of every Utah citizen.

The Brigham Young College, founded by the great pioneer whose name it bears in 1877, with an endowment of nearly 10,000 acres of the best land in the valley, is located in the heart of the city on the bank of a mountain steam of crystal water. It has a record that many older institutions might be proud of, and grows in popularity and efficiency each year. Its present building, apparatus and grounds are worth $50,000.

The district schools have modern buildings and apparatus equal to any in the territory, two recently built, the Woodruff and the Benson, costing $40,000.

Denominational schools of modern equipment and with instructors worthy the positions they hold, are conducted by the Episcopal, the Presbyterian and the Methodist churches.

The county schools, in more than twenty districts outside of Logan, have creditable buildings and are under progressive and able supervision.

DAVIS COUNTY.

The land area of Davis County may be less than that of any other County in the Territory, but there is no more important district in Utah. It lies between the eastern shore of the lake and the Wasatch mountains, between Ogden and Salt Lake City, and is traversed by the U. P. and R. G. W. Railways its entire length. Nearly the whole of its 250 square miles is under cultivation. The romantic feature of its topography is that it includes Church Island, one of the largest and most interesting islands of the Great Salt Lake. On this island there are thirty-six sections of land used for ranging purposes, a considerable portion of which is already seeded to lucern, for which it is well adapted; as also for dry farming. It is likely to be used as a summer watering place. A large proportion of the mountainous district on the main land has been taken up for range purposes. Some good timber also flourishes on these portions, but the long wide strip of land lying between the mountains and lake is exceedingly fruitful and is being cultivated to the highest degree. It is estimated that 62,400 acres of land are used for pasture, wheat, lucern, hay, barley, oats, orchards, potatoes, corn, beets and all varieties of vegetables. But little land remains subject to entry, the situation being too valuable to remain unclaimed. Cultivated land in this county is worth as high as $300 per acre, according to quality and location, the most valuable being in the market gardening district of the southern portion of the county. In the northern portion there is a considerable area of high land, on which extensive experiments in dry farming have been made with greater success than in most parts of the Territory. Davis County has done much to prove the great possibilities of farming in Utah under high cultivation. Located in a district where a ready market is assured, not only in the principal cities at home, but by reason of its railroad facilities, an extended market is open to it in the surrounding territories. There have been genuine attempts in this county to bring the land approximately to its greatest yielding power, and we doubt whether better results, quality as well as quantity considered, have ever been attained in any agricultural district in America. It is upon the southern portion of this county that Salt Lake City depends for the splendid garden produce and small fruits which come into its market early in season and throughout the summer. Figures that are hard to believe are published in California and elsewhere, as to the revenue to be derived from the cultivation of an acre in the fruitful districts of other states, but we have before us reliable data as to the revenue derived from acreage in Davis County that may well challenge comparison with the most prolific regions of America at least.

Market gardening in Bountiful, Davis County, yield per acre and average price for two years.

Lettuce	14,000	@ $ .02	per head,	$	280.00
Early Cabbage	12,000	" .05	" "		600.00
Early Cauliflower	7,260	" .10	" "		726.00
Onions	600 bu.	" .75	" bu.,		450.00
Parsnips	1,800 "	" .25	" "		450.00
Carrots	1,800 "	" .20	" "		360.00
Tomatoes	2,250 "	" .40	" "		900.00
Potatoes	350 "	" .75	" "		262.50
Large Peas	306 "	" 1.00	" "		306.00
Small Peas	200 "	" 1.25	" "		250.00
Green Beans	400 "	" .90	" "		360.00
Cucumbers	250 "	" .50	" "		125.00
Asparagus	5,500 lbs.	" .08	" lb.,		440.00
Rhubarb	7,000 "	" .01½	" "		105.00
Corn	2,420 doz.	" .10	" doz.,		242.00
Celery	30,000	" .03	" stalk,		90.00
Cantelope	1,814 doz.	" .60	" doz.,		1,088.40
Watermelons	862 "	" .40	" "		344.80

Yield per acre and highest market price in the early part of the season.

Lettuce	14,000 heads	@ $ .02½	$	310.00
Cabbage	21,000 "	" .10		120.00
Cauliflower	7,260 "	" .15		1,089.00
Onions	600 bu.	" 1.50		900.00
Parsnips	1,800 "	" .40		720.00
Carrots	1,800 "	" .25		450.00
Asparagus	5,500 lbs.	" .12½		687.50
Rhubarb	7,000 "	" .05		350.00
Corn	2,420 doz.	" .20		484.00
Tomatoes	2,250 bu.	" 2.00		4,500.00
Celery	30,000 heads	" .06		1,800.00
Cantelope	1,814 doz.	" 2.00		3,628.00
Watermelons	862 "	" 1.50		1,298.00
Large Peas	300 bu.	" 1.25		375.00
Small Peas	200 "	" 2.00		400.00
Green Beans	300 "	" 3.00		900.00
Cucumbers	350 "	" 2.00		700.00
Potatoes	350 "	" 2.00		700.00

The above figures are compiled and attested by Ephraim Briggs and Brigham Holbrook of Bountiful, Davis County, Utah.

A man having a wife and five children reports being able to make a comfortable living from an acre and a quarter of land at Bountiful.

Joseph T. Mabey gives the following statement of products per acre.

Carrots,	1500 bushels,	@ $ .22,	$	330.00
Table Beets,	1200 "	" .25,		300.00
Onions,	850 "	" .75,		637.50
Potatoes,	600 "	" .35,		210.00
Downing Gooseberries,	800 "	" 2.50,		2,000.00

Richard E. Egan has produced strawberries that yielded him $600 to the acre. A. L. Buckland, Bountiful, has realized $1,500 per acre, one year, from his strawberry patch.

E. P. Ellison at Layton, in the northern part of the county, gives the following averages:

Wheat, dry farms, 22½ bush. per acre, average price, 65c. per bush.
Wheat, irrigated, 50 bush. per acre.
Barley, dry farms, 25 to 30 bush. per acre, average price, 65c. per 100 lbs.

Barley, irrigated, 60 to 70 bush. per acre.
Oats, irrigated, 60 to 70 bush. per acre.
Lucern, best crop, 7 tons per acre, $4.50 per ton.

These figures represent averages, but authentic reports show as high as 110 bushels of oats, and 100 bushels of barley per acre.

The irrigated land of this county slopes gently south and west, and lies under the shelter of the lofty Wasatch Mountains; therefore the growing season is the longest and the climate the mildest, so that the soil can be cultivated to better advantage than any other part of the Territory. The water supply is comparatively large, the mountains supplying numerous streams and many springs appear along their base, while further water supply has been secured by tunnels driven into the flanks of the mountain range, and by flowing wells which afford a bounteous supply. The people of the county are generally well to do; real poverty is almost unknown. Davis County has thirty public schools, one private, and seven denominational schools. Much attention is being given to educational matters. The Normal College is incorporated with a capital stock of $120,000, to construct one of the largest and handsomest school buildings in the west at Bonneville, a point five miles north of Salt Lake City, and connected therewith by three different railways. The site is near the foot-hills of the Wasatch Mountains, and affords a splendid view of the valley and the Great Salt Lake. The building will be constructed of Utah stone and brick, and is intended to accommodate fifteen hundred students. The management is in the hands of J. W. Newbern, and the college has already been opened in Salt Lake City in connection with the Conservatory of Music. The undertaking is on a liberal scale, and its promoters express their determination to spare neither money nor effort to make this institution one of the most practical and popular of its kind in the United States.

The city of Bountiful is the most southerly settlement in Davis County. The population is 1,540; eight public schools, the central school house in the south precinct, being a handsome building of modern style, with approved methods of heating and ventilating, and amply supplied with furniture and school appliances. It has a library and collection of specimens in natural history. Centerville, Farmington, Kaysville and Syracuse, also have excellent educational institutions. The climate is essentially the same as that of Salt Lake Valley. Although some undeveloped mining claims exist in the mountains along the edge of the county, but little attention has been given to the subject. The principal mineral resource is the salt industry maintained along the shore of the Great Salt Lake, near the line of the Union Pacific and Rio Grande Western Railways.

But Davis County is famous as the location of the wonderful wells of Natural Gas that have been developed by the New American Gas and Fuel Company. There are five wells completed and ready to turn into mains, showing the following pressure per inch and capacity of flow in twenty-four hours as measured by standard gauge; also depth of wells:

No. 1, depth, 780 feet, 200 lbs. pressure, flows 4,900,700 feet.
No. 2,   "   760 "   190 lbs.   "   "   3,200,000 "
No. 3,   "   792 "   200 lbs.   "   "   4,000,000 "
No. 4,   "   808 "   240 lbs.   "   "   2,500,000 "
No. 5,   "   820 "   250 lbs.   "   "   5,500,000 "

                                                    20,100,700 "
2 small wells that flow 800,000 feet each, . . .   1,600,000 "

            Total, . . . 21,700,700 cubic feet.

These wells are all cased with wrought iron pipe from the surface to the gas deposit. The drives pass through large bodies of black shale and soapstone before the gas rock is reached. The gas is found in a very porous grey

THE COUNTIES OF UTAH. 63

sandstone. The difference of flow in the several wells is caused by the hardness or softness of the rock where the gas is tapped. The company own and control something over 6,000 acres of land in the gas fields. These wells are situated twelve miles north of Salt Lake City, and about twenty miles south of Ogden. The Union Pacific and Rio Grande Western railroads both pass through these fields. It is a question of only a short time until manufactories will take advantage of this cheap fuel and make Davis County the leading county of the Great West. Raw material of many kinds, including iron, lay contiguous to the wells. The developments in the gas field were commenced about March, 1892, but a large spring showing gas "which can be lighted," has been known to exist for more than forty years near the center of this great Natural Gas field.

It has been said with good reason that a glass factory and a beet sugar factory (the land is well adapted to raising sugar beets) and other industries might be established in this neighborhood, and that power for the same could be derived from the Weber Canal.

The manufacture of brick is one of the thriving industries of Davis County. There are two banks in the county, the Barnes Banking Company of Kaysville, and the Davis County Bank at Farmington, the county seat. The Layton Roller Mills, the Star Mills at Farmington, and the Thistle Mills at Kaysville, produce excellent flour, while several creameries exist in the different settlements. The Woods Cross Canning and Pickling Company is actively engaged in developing this branch of industry.

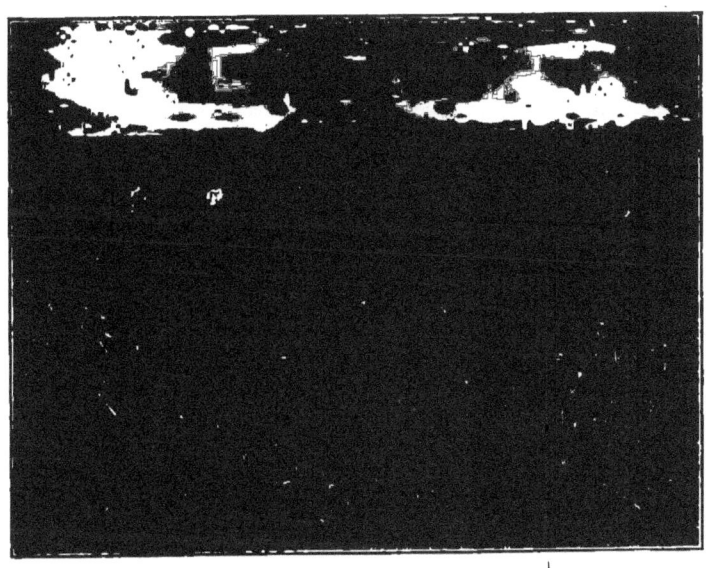

TIMOTHY HAY FIELD.

EMERY COUNTY.

Emery County lies along the Rio Grande Western Railway, in the middle-eastern part of the Territory. It is drained by Green River, the principal fork of the Colorado. About 20,000 acres are under cultivation, the greater part of which is irrigated, and a much larger area will shortly be under cultivation, as au abundance of water can be taken from Green River and more can be stored in the mountains to the westward. This will require considerable outlay, which, however, will yield ample returns for the investment. The county seat is Castle Dale, one of the farming settlements of the central portion of the county; but a more important point is the town of Price, an active shipping point from which supplies are distributed to Fort Duchesne, Vernal, and other places to the north, and also to the farming districts to the south. All of the gilsonite produced in the Duchesne valley reaches the railway at this point, and Price has therefore become something of a commercial center. The town of Helper is an active railway town, and the great coal fields of Pleasant Valley are situated in the north-west corner of Emery County. A considerable business is done in lumbering, in charcoal burning and in the coke industry. The population of the county is about seven thousand and the assessed valuation $2,040,812. A very large area of the best cattle and sheep raising country is comprised within this county, the high mesas affording excellent feed in summer and the lower valleys constituting one of the best winter ranges in the Territory.

GARFIELD COUNTY.

This county is situated in the central-southern part of the Territory in the midst of the wild, weird mountains and plateaus that drain into the Colorado. It is but sparsely settled, remote from travel and comparatively undeveloped. Only a couple of thousand acres are under cultivation, but these yield high average crops. Barley, for instance, produces on the average fifty-two bushels to the acre against an average for the Territory of only twenty-nine bushels. Other cereals are produced in proportion. The county is composed for the most part of high plateaus and mountain ranges, deeply cut canyons, which rarely open to a sufficient width for agricultural operations; but the county is well adapted for sheep and cattle raising, especially in winter. In the western portion of the county, however, along the east and the west forks of the Sevier, there are several thriving farming towns, among them, Panguitch and Orton, and the country there is more open and suitable for cultivation. A year or two ago much attention was directed to the eastern portion of Garfield County by the Henry Mountain gold excitement. It was sufficiently proven that paying placer fields existed in this region, but its remoteness and the difficulty of procuring water, except by heavy outlays, have been the principal reasons why this excitement has subsided.

GRAND COUNTY.

Grand County adjoins Colorado in the middle eastern part of the Territory. It was but little known until it was traversed by the Rio Grande Western railway on its course. It is sparsely populated and but little developed. The Grand River runs through it, but as yet only a limited area has been cultivated. Its principal use at present is for range purposes, but several small settlements, such as Moab and Richardson on the Grand River, have proven the fruitfulness of the county. Not only grain is raised, but the orchards and vineyards are remarkably productive. Only 3850 acres are under cultivation, but five hundred thousand acres are reported as open for reclamation, while two and a half millions of acres are suitable for range and pasture. A great agricultural future is undoubtedly in store for Grand County, and it will probably become the principal corn producing district of the Territory. 245 acres are in orchards, and a shipping business of no mean proportions has already begun, from Thompson's Station, of peaches, apples, apricots, plums, pears and honey, sent in boxes to the mining districts of Colorado and to Salt Lake City. The report includes a product of 12,500 lbs. of honey, twenty-five gallons of wine, 375 hives of bees and 75,000 pounds of wool shipped, and an export of nearly 5,000 cattle and horses, and over 1,000 sheep. Shipments from this county have also been made of asphaltum, agates, ores and minerals of 40,000 pounds. Such activity as this maintained by a population of not over 750 people indicates that Grand County, with its splendid ranges and pastures, watered by the great rivers of the Grand and Green, will develop very rapidly, and at this time it probably offers as good inducements for settlement as any other county in the Territory.

IRON COUNTY.
BY W. R. M'BRIDE.

IT is situated in the south western part of Utah. Its area is about 3,400 square miles, a large portion of which is now being utilized for grazing purposes. The great Escalante desert on the west, covering an area of 345,600 acres, affords winter quarters for thousands of cattle, horses and sheep, returning to the Wasatch Mountains on the east in the spring-time, where they remain during the summer subsisting upon the nutritious grass and sparkling waters of this beautiful range. The fine pasturage afforded by the native bunch-grass and other hardy varieties that cover the mountain slopes and even the great desert, has made stock-raising a valuable industry in Iron County. Great numbers of horses and cattle are driven or shipped eastward every year, and with the thousands of pounds of wool exported annually furnish one of the most important sources of revenue to the county. The Wasatch Mountains along the eastern border of the county, densely covered with large forest trees, afford every facility for the production of millions of feet of lumber, accessible to the inhabitants of the valleys. Another charming feature of this mountain region is the many beautiful summer resorts. Panguitch Lake is a splendid body of clear crystal water situated at the top of the range, fifteen miles east of Parowan City. The settled portion of the county lies along the western base of the mountains, a distance of fifty miles. The cities of Iron County are Parowan, Cedar, Paragonah, Kanarra, Summit, Enoch, and Hamilton's Fort. Parowan, the county seat, population about 1,200, is situated in the central part of the county, near the base of the Wasatch Mountains. It is built on elevated land, making it an observatory to the great Parowan Valley, in which are the towns Paragonah and Summit. Cedar City is nineteen miles south of Parowan, in the Rush Lake Valley, population 1,500. It is one of the leading cities of southern Utah and may become the metropolis of the territory. Its location is favorable in every respect, being adjacent to large deposits of coal, and the most extensive iron fields in the world. It is midway between Denver, Colorado and Los Angeles, California, hence the right place for a large city. The entire people of the county are intelligent, generous, and hospitable, and are in good financial condition. The people at large take a great interest in the cause of education. Aside from the district school, the county has three church schools. The chief pursuits of the people are farming and stock raising.

In Iron County there are 225,860 acres of surveyed tillable land, 22,000 acres under cultivation, 201,860 acres subject to homestead and desert entry, and 2,000 acres entered, but not patented. This land is very productive. All that is now under cultivation is well irrigated. Parowan Valley, situated in the north-eastern part of the county, will no doubt, become the agricultural stronghold of the county. It is comparatively level, sloping gradually from the Wasatch Mountains on the east to the hills on the west. At the base of these hills is found the inland sea of southern Utah—Little Salt Lake, five miles in length by three-fourths of a mile in width. Parowan Valley is twenty-five miles long by ten miles wide, extending north-east and south-west. Its soil is very fertile, producing wheat, oats, barley, potatoes, hay, fruit and vegetables. All the land in the valley can be utilized for agricultural purposes by means of reservoiring and artesian wells, the latter now being used very extensively. The estimated flow of water is fifteen gallons per minute at a depth of forty-five]feet. The opportunities for building reservoirs are numerous and extensive, making it possible for the uplands at the foot of the mountains to be irrigated; in consequence of which the lowlands sub-irrigate, making very profitable hay ground. Rush Lake Valley, forty-five miles long by ten wide, lies immediately south and west of Parowan Valley. In this valley are found the thriving towns of Kanarra, Enoch, Hamilton Fort and Cedar City. The land is well watered and exceedingly productive. The North-east Canal & Reservoir Company are taking out a canal from Coal Creek, near Cedar City, which will carry sufficient water to irrigate 2,400 acres of upland, and 1,000 acres of hay land.

The average price of cultivated land throughout the county is $25.00 per acre. Its chief products are alfalfa, wheat, oats, barley, potatoes and apples. Alfalfa predominates; five tons to the acre are produced yearly, selling at $5.00 per ton. The average yield of wheat is thirty bushels per acre at $1.00 per hundred weight, and of oats thirty-five bushels per acre at $1.00 per hundred weight.

Owing to the elevation of Iron County, its situation between the lofty rain barriers of the Sierra Nevada on the west, and the Wasatch range on the east, and its generally mountainous character, its atmosphere is light, dry, clear and invigorating. Notwithstanding there is a great variation in temperature, the climate in all parts is very salubrious. In summer it is agreeably cool and refreshing in the upper valleys, mild in the lower, and decidedly warm near the desert tracts. The fall of snow in winter is light in the lower valleys, but deep in the mountain canyons and upper valleys, furnishing a large supply of water for irrigating.

Coal and iron deposits are abundant. They are all found in the southern part of the county, with the exception of a heavy vein of iron ore lying immediately north of Little Creek canyon near Paragoonah in Parowan Valley. Small veins of coal are also found in this vicinity, and some traces of gold and silver.

The great coal fields extending from Cedar City on the north to the town of Kanarra on the south, and as far east as the Colorado, are inexhaustible and superior in quality. Two thousand acres of these coal lands are now being developed in Cedar Canyon. This field is second to none in quantity and quality. Some of it cokes very readily and is therefore very valuable for smelting purposes. In fact it has already been tested on Iron County iron ore, both magnetic and hematite, with gratifying success. It is sufficient in quantity to supply the entire Pacific slope with coal for furnaces and domestic purposes. As soon as the Nevada Southern railroad is built, (and it is coming this way as fast as possible,) capital will follow, huge furnaces will be built, and from Iron County will go the manufactured iron and steel to be consumed in the hundreds of industries in our great and growing west. This railroad enterprise, the market thus opened for our coal, and the assured establishment of iron works, will make a Pittsburg of Cedar City and a Pennsylvania of Iron County.

Iron exists in a belt extending from Iron Springs on the north, eight miles from Cedar City, to Iron City on the south, a distance of fifteen miles, with an average width of three miles, culminating in Iron Mountain, towering 1,500 feet above the level of the valley. This deposit is estimated to be ninety per cent pure iron. This vast area of iron ore is a monument to the world, inexhaustible in its nature, unsurpassed in quality and containing millions upon millions of hidden treasure, and, as Captain Foxwell says: "If all the lumber in the world, and all the buildings were destroyed, and if all the buildings during the the world's existence had to be constructed of iron, there is one mountain in Utah which would furnish enough iron for the world."

This mountain is in Iron County.

JUAB COUNTY.

THIS county, situated in the centre of the western side of the Territory, consists of a long narrow strip, extending westward from the Wasatch Mountains across the desert to the Nevada line. The greater portion of the western district is almost entirely without water and a part of it is covered by the Great Salt Lake Desert; nevertheless it affords winter range for innumerable sheep, which are able to find moisture sufficient for their needs among the gorges of the desert ranges which break across the plains in lines from north to south at intervals but a few miles apart. Not only does the arid region contribute in this manner towards the wealth of the sheep owners, but in these desert ranges already mentioned there are mines which will undoubtedly contribute largely in the future towards the mineral output of the Territory. In the Dugway, Fish Springs and Deep Creek mining districts are numberless lodes of lead, silver, gold and copper that have attracted the attention of mining speculators for a great many years, and but for the lack of transportation facilities, would long since have been developed into perhaps the most important mineral producing region of the Territory. To secure the building of a railroad to these regions many attempts have been made by local capitalists, but so far, without avail; yet the conviction is deep in the minds of all that sooner or later a railroad will enable those who have persistantly held on to these claims to prove their value, and many fortunes will be reaped. Enormous deposits are there reported, their proportions almost surpassing belief; but they are mostly low grade and will not bear the wagon haul. Thorough investigations have been made at various times and the tonnage that these mines would secure to a railway passing through that part of the country, would undoubtedly furnish sufficient traffic for its support. The eastern part of the county however, is of an entirely different character, well watered by numerous streams, and a great part of its area has been under cultivation for many years. The celebrated Tintic mining district, into which the Rio Grande Western Railway has recently built one of its most important spurs, has been one of the greatest producers of the Territory. The Bullion-Beck, Eureka-Hill, Mammoth and other famous mines have yielded fortune upon fortune to their lucky possessors. But besides the mining of the noble metals there are iron mines, gypsum, saltpetre, graphite, salt and other minerals, many of which are being produced with profit and contribute to the mineral output of the Territory. The county seat is Nephi, which has been called the "Little Chicago" by its enterprising inhabitants. It is certainly among the most important towns south of Salt Lake City, and a prominent shipping point for wool and other exports. .Here the Nephi Plaster Works are engaged in manufacturing a first class article of Plaster of Paris, with which they not only supply the entire demand in Utah, but annually ship many carloads to California. Their exhibit will be prominent in the Utah department at the Midwinter Fair. Salt springs and great reefs of rock salt, also in the neighborhood of Nephi, afford the means of sustaining two active and successful producers of dairy salt of singular purity, besides which great quantities of rock salt for stock purposes are shipped throughout the inter-mountain region. Nephi supports a bank and a number of important mercantile institutions. Among its enterprising citizens are some who are engaged in the development of asphalt fields and other resources of the Territory; but the principal support of the county are the ranch and range interests, and the products of the agricultural districts throughout the valley. The highest peak of the Wasatch Mountains, Mount Nebo, 12 000 feet, lies just back of Nephi and is a conspicuous feature of the country. Levan, Mona, Juab and other towns are the centres of the agricultural regions. The assessed valuation of the county is $2,427,328., but it must be remembered that the mining properties are not subject to assessment. These have a value of many millions.

KANE COUNTY.

This county adjoins Arizona on the central-southern portion of the Territory, but is remote from travel and its population does not exceed 2,000. A few towns, Kanab, Glendale, Mount Carmel and one or two others exist on the head waters of the Rio Virgin and other streams which flow into the Colorado River. The greater part of the county consists of plateaus, suitable for sheep ranges, but the streams flow through deep gorges cut through the alluvial soil at such depths that the water cannot be diverted to the main land. The scenery of this region is wild and romantic, and full of interest to the explorer, yet this feature does not contribute to its prosperity. The valleys to which water can be brought are narrow, limiting the arable land; but in such places farms are very fruitful and the yield is correspondingly high. The assessed valuation of the county in 1893 was $732,520, but the live stock owned by its inhabitants is worth not less than half a million.

MILLARD COUNTY.

This is a large county in the southwest part and, in the early history of the Territory, was the county seat, and Fillmore was the capital city of the Territory for several years. Out of 400,000 acres of tillable land, about one-quarter is under cultivation, the remainder being unoccupied and subject to entry. But fully one half of the western portion is desert and suitable only for winter range. Cultivated land is worth from $20 to $50 per acre, lying along the valley of the Sevier and on the western slopes of the Wasatch Range. Good reservoir opportunities exist which might materially increase the cultivated area. It has been estimated that at least 100,000 acres not now used for farming could by these means be settled up. The largest yields reported to the acre are five tons of hay, fifty bushels of wheat, fifty five bushels of oats, one hundred bushels of barley and 500 bushels of potatoes. The climate is temperate and cattle and all kinds of grazing stock do well. It is a region to which hundreds of thousands of sheep are driven in the winter, a circumstance which contributes as much to the good fortune of sheep raisers from other counties as to the well-being of the inhabitants of Millard County. In the spurs of the Wasatch Mountains and in some of the desert ranges a number of mines have been discovered, although but little worked. The famous black onyx which has recently commanded much attention, is produced in this county, and arrangements have been made to ship it by the carload to the east. Nothing to rival this beautiful stone has so far been discovered in America. Lead, silver, gold and copper seem to predominate, and promise to make the mining interests of the county important in the future. Fillmore, Kanosh, Scipio, Deseret and other towns supply a thriving farming population. The residents of the county number over 4,000: the assessed valuation last year was $1,678,947. The Union Pacific Railway passes through the county, affording means of transportation for its products and its requirements. Cattle and sheep constitute its principal exports.

MORGAN COUNTY.

This little county occupies a district through which the Union Pacific Railway passes, between Ogden and Echo. It is extremely mountainous in character, but the Weber Valley with its several towns, Morgan, Peterson and Croyden, is a delightful relief, and the limited amount of land which there is under cultivation yields good returns. Wheat, oats, barley, potatoes and some small fruit, are the principal products, and of these over 7,000 acres are under the plow. The towns being within easy reach of Ogden and Salt Lake City the produce of the county is easily marketed at good figures. Cultivated land is worth $75 and more per acre. Of late years many silver producing claims have been recorded and some ore has been shipped. With the restoration in the price of silver and lead, further developments would begin at once. Some gold prospects have also been discovered. The population is about 2,000 and the assessed valuation about $600,000.

PIUTE COUNTY.

This is one of the small counties of the Territory in the south central part. It is almost wholly covered by high mountains, the Wasatch at this point reaching an altitude of nearly 12,000 feet. But for its distance from railway communication, Piute County would become prominent for its mines, some of the most promising properties being located near Marysvale. Gold, silver, lead and copper will some day be produced there in great quantities. At this point also quicksilver has been produced in paying quantities, the output for one year being over $7,000. From an agricultural point of view this county is not conspicuous, but nevertheless some 2,500 people derive sustenance therefrom, the water being in abundance and the soil fruitful.

RICH COUNTY.

This county lies in the northeast corner of Utah. It is not very large but it is nearly all agricultural land. Thirty thousand acres are cultivated or in pasture, the tributaries of Bear River furnishing an abundance of water. The elevation of Bear Valley is about 7,000 feet, rendering the climate somewhat cold, but the hardier crops flourish. A beautiful feature of the northern part of this county is Bear Lake, a magnificent sheet of water about fifteen miles in width by thirty or forty in length. This is one of the largest bodies of fresh water that exist at such elevation in the mountain regions, and is the natural reservoir upon which the great Bear River canal depends for its permanent summer supply. The scenic features of this portion of the county are exceedingly attractive, and some of the towns lying along the shore of the lake are almost wholly supported by trout fishing, supplying the markets of several territories with large and splendid fish. The lake is deep, wonderfully clear and a marvel of beautiful color. At the southern end are Laketown, Meadowville and other thriving farming settlements, while along the eastern bank of the lake at points where the mountains recede from the shore the recesses are occupied by some of the most delightful farms in the Territory. The population of the county, however, is not great, though the people are generally well to do, owing to the success which usually attends their stock raising enterprises.

SALT LAKE COUNTY.

Even if Salt Lake County did not enjoy the distinction of possessing the capital city of the Territory, it would rival the most important of other counties in many ways. A portion of its cultivated ground at least, is as fertile as any land in any country on the face of the earth. The results of actual cultivation justify this statement. Greater and better crops have never been raised in America than on the farms which lie to the southward of Salt Lake City. This extremely fertile district is comparatively limited, and there are large stretches of land on the western portion of the valley which have not yet been proven to be so productive. From a scenic point of view the magnificent front of the Wasatch Mountains as seen overlooking the valley, has been pronounced by great artists like Bierstadt and Moran, the finest which our continent affords. Among the rocky passes of this range are other beautiful scenes, alpine lakes, snowy peaks, stretches of forest and beautiful nooks which afford delightful and healthful recreation to those who explore them throughout the summer months; and among the heights of the Wasatch as well as in the canyons of the Oquirrh which bounds the valley on the west, millions of dollars worth of gold and silver, lead and copper, have been mined to add to the prosperity and wealth of the citizens of the county. The marvelous Great Salt Lake, famous among all travelers, is another feature of the valley, and its unequalled bathing affords a principal source of pleasure to its people. The challenge has been offered, but never taken up, that no scene in the world affords so many elements of beauty to the spectator as that beheld from the heights above Salt Lake City. The population of the county is set at 67,000, the greater part of them residents of the capital city. Salt Lake County has an area of only 784 square miles, but it is an empire within itself, and the centre of interest to the whole Territory. It has more manufacturing interests located within its boundaries than all the rest of the inter-mountain country combined, and has an assessed valuation of $48,467,854. Although its manufacturing and commercial interests predominate, the agricultural features of the county are by no means insignificant. Over 27,000 acres of land are under irrigation, and 30,000 under cultivation, and generally speaking, it is high cultivation. Besides this, there are 15,000 acres used for pasture. The agricultural yield is valued at $792,242. On the day that the Mormons first entered the valley, July 24, 1847, the first furrow was plowed in the Great Basin, and that year the agricultural possibilities of Utah were demonstrated. No valley in all the arid regions surpasses this in its natural facilities for irrigation. The water supply comes from the various streams which issue from the Wasatch Mountains into the valley, and from the Jordan River which flows from Utah Lake; and the whole area of the eastern side of the valley is one vast net-work of canals and ditches. The development of this system of irrigation has accumulated moisture in the soil, so that a far larger area is now cultivated than appeared possible in the early history of the valley. As stated in the article on agriculture, it was on the outskirts of Salt Lake City that the climax of wheat production in America was reached, in a yield of over 80 bushels to the acre. The kinds of crops have the greatest acreage in the following order: lucern, wheat, hay, barley, potatoes, corn, rye, orchards, beets and vineyards. Other farm products consist of butter, honey, dried fruits, vinegar, cider and wine. The county has large interests in cattle, horses and sheep. The towns and cities outside of Salt Lake are Big Cottonwood, Brighton, Bingham, Mill Creek, Granger, Hunter, North Jordan, Pleasant Green, Sugar House, South Cottonwood, the City of Sandy, South Jordan, Union and West Jordan. A great enterprise now under way is the Big Cottonwood Power & Water Co., with a capital stock of $1,000,000, organized to use the waters of Big Cottonwood Creek, for the generation of electric power for general use, chiefly in Salt Lake City. The principal smelters in the mountain country are located in the valley about ten miles south of the city; they consist of the Hanauer, Mingo and Germania smelters and Refinery, and are usually in full operation, smelting the ores of many mining districts in this Territory and a great deal that are brought from Idaho and Nevada. The metallic output of these works in 1893 was $3,623,537.96.

SALT LAKE CITY.

Salt Lake City, the capital of Utah Territory, is the beautiful metropolis of the inter-mountain country, and its singular history as the Zion of the Mormons has made it known throughout the world. It was the first city to be settled in the western part of the continent, and was well known before Denver was first thought of. Passing over all ancient history, however, the vital interests of Salt Lake City as they exist today, can scarcely be described in the limited space at our disposal in these pages; yet many of the salient facts relating thereto are at least indicated in the articles throughout this work, because whether Utah is discussed as to its climate, agriculture, commerce, industries or social conditions, the interests of Salt Lake City play an important part in whatever aspect they are considered. The city itself has a population of about 60,000. It rests upon a gentle slope, facing to the south and west, at the base of the Wasatch Mountains. Its streets are 132 feet wide and in the central part are paved with Belgian blocks and Utah asphaltum. They all run north and south

and east and west. Five and six story business blocks, built of stone and equipped with all modern conveniences, constitute the greater portion of the business part of the city. These are thoroughly metropolitan in design and appointments. Street after street is lined with business houses, many of which absorb a large volume of trade. Every line of business is well represented and a large jobbing trade is done, an extensive region in every direction being tributary to the capital of the Territory. Sixteen banks with an aggregate capital of $6,000,000 compass the financial requirements of the city; they have a clearing house whose clearings in 1893 were $58,456,129, the volume of business being maintained with regularity throughout the year. This unerring guide to the business activity of a city thus proclaims that with the exception of San Francisco, Cal., and Portland, Oregon, Salt Lake City is the most important business centre west of the Rocky Mountains. It is also a great educational centre. Seven hundred and fifty thousand dollars has been spent during the past two years on our public schools. As Mr. W. E. Hubbard stated on retiring at the end of last year from the Presidency of the Chamber of Commerce, "No true American can ride through our city, noting the beautiful and capacious buildings, of most approved architecture, noting also their number, and fail to be filled with pride at the opportunities afforded the young of this community. The corps of teachers consists of the best native and imported talent, who have perfected a system on most approved lines, and fully abreast with the best educational centres. Our school board deserves especial commendation for the minute attention given to the details of light, heat and ventilation. The poor cannot plead inability to educate their children on account of the expense of books and supplies, for these are generously furnished them gratis."

The corporation expended on city improvements last year $739,000 The city and county building, nearing completion, built of Utah kyune sandstone, at a cost of $550,000, is a model of architecture, and a new and beautiful feature among our public buildings. Although we have one sewerage system, a gravity sewer is being constructed at a cost of $300,000, which will continue to keep our city the healthiest in the United States, as the records for the past two years have shown it to be. $20,000 was spent last year on our sidewalks, and $250,000 on street paving. Two rival electric street railway companies furnish rapid transit to all parts of the city and to the suburbs. One of them has forty-two miles of track and operates about sixty cars; the other has thirty-three miles of track and a proportionate equipment. The splendid water system is owned by the city and valued today at $1,500,000. The city fire department is a model of effectiveness. The famous Salt Lake Temple, costing $5,000 000, built of white granite, is one of the grandest structures in America; the great Mormon Tabernacle, with a seating capacity of 10,000, is also widely famed. A number of fine hotels with all modern conveniences, accommodate the traveling public. Salt Lake City possesses many unique features that are attractive to the tourist and are a theme of interest to the thousands who remain over at all seasons to examine them; but during the past few years it has attracted less attention as the Zion of the Mormons than as the active, prosperous, business center of the western commonwealth. In and out of Salt Lake City the two great western railways have fetched and carried for many years the great bulk of the local traffic of the Territory; importing all the varied supplies for the wants of hundreds of thousands of people, and taking away train loads of ore, and a vast tonnage of bullion, grain, hides and wool, manufactures and general merchandise. Salt Lake City is one of the great tourist resorts of America, and its celebrated bathing places attract thousands to stay there during the summer. During the period of financial and business prostration which affected the whole country in 1893, there was no city which escaped its effects more than Salt Lake. Not a bank closed its doors, and no business failures of any importance took place. The real estate sales of last year amounted to $6,500,000. In the graces of civilization, music, fine arts and literature, Salt Lake City is in advance of any other western city. Associations devoted separately to these matters not only exist, but flourish, commanding the attention and respect of the whole country and adding refinement to the many other advantages of life in the mountain metropolis.

The sanitary advantages of the thermal and medicinal springs which exist within the city limits have received much attention. One of the principal efforts in this direction is that of the Salt Lake Hot Springs Sanitarium Company, organized in 1892, with a capital of $150,000. It is built in the heart of the city, a sanitarium and bathing resort second to none in the world. It is a fine commodious building with a floor space of about 50,000 square feet. The water, at a temperature of 112 degrees, is drawn from the hot sulphur springs on the northern outskirts of the city, with a flow of about 400 gallons per minute, conducted to the heart of the city through an eight-inch pipe line, entering the establishment at a temperature of 110 degrees Fahr. Besides large separate swimming pools for men and women, there are twelve private pools and a number of elegant private bath-rooms furnished with porcelain bath-tubs. A hotel and gymnasium are connected with the enterprise in the same building. The medicinal properties of the water consist chiefly of common salt, epsom salt, glauber's salt and various sulphates. The baths are an acknowledged cure for nervousness, catarrh, rheumatism, dyspepsia and other diseases; taken internally the waters are a specific for a greater number of afflictions. The advantages of Wasatka mineral water, another famous city spring, are described under the head of mineral resources.

It is in the volume and variety of its manufacturing interests that Salt Lake City maintains its principal importance. There are about one hundred manufacturing concerns in about fifty different lines, with a capital invested of over two million dollars, and an annual product of about three millions. Among the various articles of commerce manufactured are boots and shoes, show-cases, cigars, knit goods, soap, paper boxes, machinery and boilers, trunks, leather, overalls, clothing, fire brick, flour and other mill products, tents, carriages, beer, crackers, soda water, copperware, rope, woolen goods, silk, etc. There are also a number of foundries, printing offices, book binderies, turning shops, planing and wood working mills, stone yards, lime-kilns and big asphalt works, the great copper plant described in our general article on the industries of Utah, large cement works, saddlery shops, salt works, creameries, meat packing houses, an artificial ice factory, wire works, etc. The Salt Lake Pressed Brick Company, after three years of push and energy, and with an investment of over $60,000 have succeeded in producing a red shade of brick, beautiful in color and wonderful in strength. One of its bricks stood a hydraulic pressure of 240,000 pounds This concern can now supply the demands with fine facing brick, displacing previous importations from the east, and is now shipping its product to Denver; Leavenworth; Kansas; Butte, Montana; and all interior points. Their exhibition was awarded a gold medal at the World's Fair, and has secured two gold medals from our Territorial Fairs. The capacity is 80,000 bricks per day, made with two Boyd presses.

Putting together the commerce and industries of Salt Lake City, the capital invested in 1890 was $14,500,000; the sales amounted to $30,000,000; and the wages paid annually were nearly $4,000,000.

SAN JUAN COUNTY.

San Juan County occupies a vast district in the south-east corner of the Territory—a wild region, the last to be explored among the mountains of the west; yet even here, settlement has already begun along the fruitful river bottoms, which drain into the San Juan and the Colorado. South of the San Juan, with the exception of a little strip near the Colorado, it is occupied by the Navajos for their reservation. In the southern part of the county the high and mountainous region is well covered with long-leaf pine, cedar and pinyon pine. The greater part of the county, however, consists of high plateaus, frequently divided by deep and impassable gorges cut through the soft sandstone to a depth of thousands of feet. The great San Juan River half a mile wide, cuts through this country, with perpendicular cliffs several hundred feet in height. The river bottom is sandy and the stream sluggish, and owing to its sudden and extreme rises and changes in its course it is almost impossible to utilize any portion of it for irrigation. A number of locations have been made, however, along its course and much money has been expended in attempting to control its waters for farming, which have usually failed, except at Bluff City where some 200 acres are under cultivation, watered from a canal which has cost $60,000 to construct. This would seem unprofitable farming, but it is absolutely essential to the residence of the settlers, who are extensively engaged in stock raising. Five or six other running streams traverse the county, and where these are not too closely shut in by the cliffs on either side of the river, are appropriated and used by small farmers. Although the altitude at Bluff City is only 4,500 feet, the extremes of temperature are reported at 110 degrees in summer to fourteen degrees below zero in winter, a singular exception to the equable climate characteristic of the Territory in general. There is but little snow fall, however, in San Juan County, except in the high mountains. At the town of Monticello the altitude is 7,500 feet, and the snow fall there is much greater. Notwithstanding its remoteness, the difficulty of securing water and its other disadvantages, the settlers have actually produced a fair supply of apples, peaches, pears, currants, grapes, sugar cane, lucern and all sorts of garden products, and are hopeful of still further increasing the volume of their agricultural output. The mountains have been but little explored for mineral, but large supplies of iron, marble, onyx, lime and lithographing stone, lead and copper, have been revealed; silver in lesser quantity, and a gold excitement which prevailed in the neighborhood a year or two ago attracted hundreds of fortune seekers, who found the much coveted metal in limited quantities but could not maintain their operations under such adverse circumstances.

SANPETE COUNTY.

There is no more delightful or interesting valley in the whole Territory than Sanpete, in the central part, and none which has maintained more continuous prosperity since the settlement of the country. It is about one hundred miles south of Salt Lake City, and the valley has an altitude of nearly 6,000 feet. The climate is delicious, bright and sunny, and it is probably the most fertile and productive valley in the whole inter-mountain region. Sanpete Valley has rivalled Cache Valley in its claim to be the granary of Utah, and is probably entitled to the name, because it was the first to achieve a right to the title. There are 50,000 acres in this valley under cultivation, and twice as much more can be considered tillable. The price of land here is $25 to $50 per acre. Wheat and oats furnish the principal crops, the output being not less than a quarter of a million bushels per annum, year in and year out. Out of a population of 15,000 people, five-sixths of them are engaged in agricultural pursuits. The Sanpitch River traverses the valley, affording with its beautiful tributaries, an abundance of water for irrigation, although numerous drive wells furnish a still further supply. The importance of this county will be realized by its assessed valuation, which is $4,429,600, and a very few statistics will make this still more clear:

It has 6,000 head of horses and mules, 1,000 head of cattle, 350,000 sheep. One wool company alone has shipped from Manti, the county seat, to Boston, during the past season, 2,500,000 pounds of wool, and the annual shipments of sheep for the past five years have been from 40,000 to 60,000 head. Farms yield to the acre, forty bushels of wheat, fifty bushels of oats, sixty bushels of barley, 250 bushels of potatoes, while the garden products such as carrots, beets, radishes, onions, etc., are prolific. Such fruits as apples, pears, plums, apricots, gooseberries, currants and strawberries grow to perfection. The streams

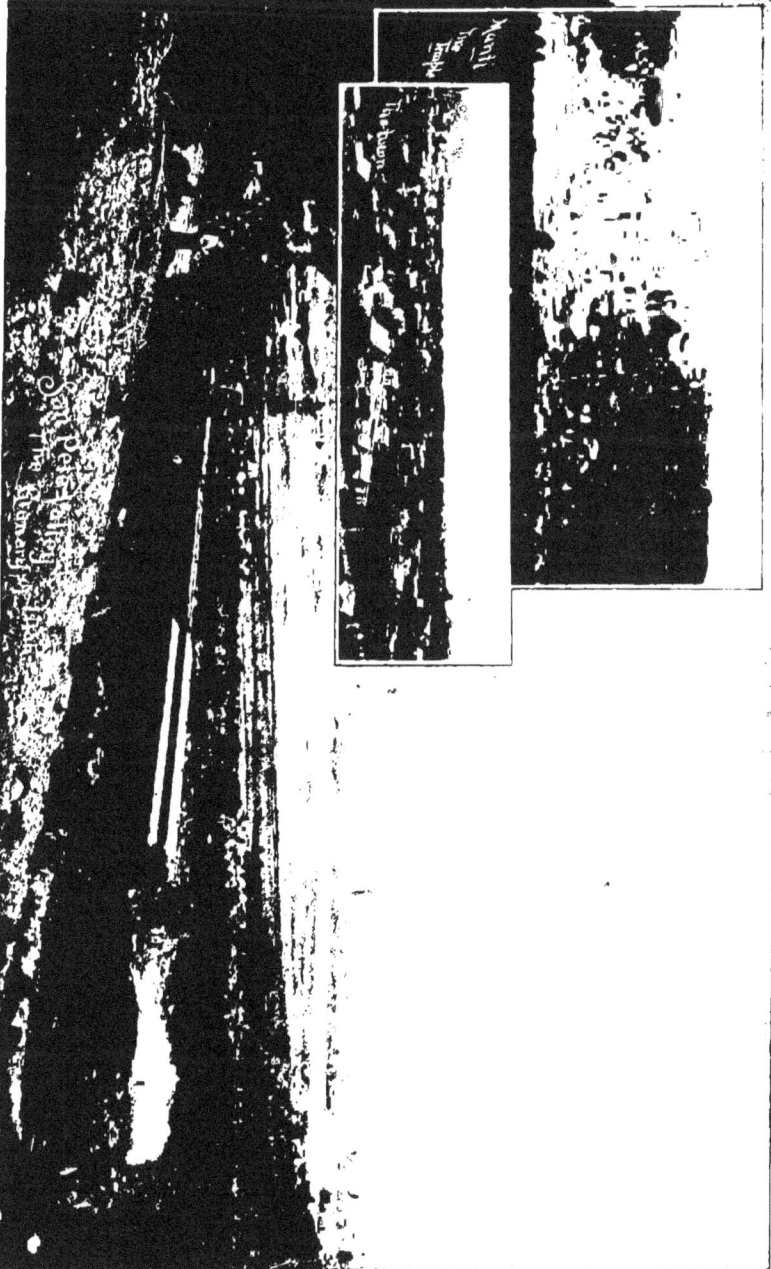

which dash down from the Wasatch Mountains in the east of the valley, not only supply the farms with irrigation water but furnish power for about thirty mills in the canyons; and the pine forests of the Wasatch and Sanpitch mountains make lumber plenty and cheap, the present price being $15.00 per thousand feet. The beautiful oolite sandstone of which the Manti Temple is built is a cheap and popular structural material for the residents of the valley. Abundance of coal and fire wood exist in many places and are exported to the neighboring valleys. Reservoir opportunities are to be found in many places. The Rio Grande western Railway runs the entire length of the valley, passing through Indianola, Milburn, Fairview, Mount Pleasant, Spring City, Ephraim, Manti, Sterling and onward to the south. Another line is the Sanpete Valley Railway, a narrow gauge road, leaving the Union Pacific at Nephi in Juab County, and on reaching Sanpete County passes through Fountain Green, Moroni, Chester, Freedom, Wales and Ephraim to Manti, its present terminus. Among the mineral resources of the county, fine prospects of silver and lead have been opened in the west mountains, while salt, gypsum, lime, ochre, asphaltum, fire-clay, brick-clay, alum, saltpetre and other minerals abound in the county. The capital of Sanpete County is Manti, settled in 1849, situated at the foot-hills of the Wasatch Mountains on the east side of the valley. Its population is 3,000, and it has fine school houses and a number of good stores. The beautiful Manti Temple, a marvel of architectural grace and dainty in color and design, and indeed one of the greatest of the Mormon Temples, is here located on a point of a hill seventy feet above the level of the town, and is a conspicuous feature of the landscape as seen from many miles to the north or south. Manti is proud of its fish ponds and of its warm springs, its clear atmosphere and romantic scenery, and very justly claims to be a sanitarium. Ephraim is an important town in the county a few miles north of Manti, with a population of 2,700, and with nearly all of its homes built of solid stone. Spring City is again a few miles further to the north. Mount Pleasant is the second city of the county in importance. It has a bank, good schools, hotels, a newspaper, well built homes, flourishing farms and enterprising citizens. Fairview, Milburn, Chester, Wales, Freedom, Fountain Green, Sterling and Mayfield resemble each other in their principal attributes of thrift, and that their inhabitants are happy and contented in the midst of plenty. No such thing as actual poverty, is known throughout the county. The average wealth of the citizens may not be great in money, but they all have the means of sustaining a comfortable livelihood and many of them are nabobs in a small way and are surrounded by all the comforts of life and many of its luxuries. Their lives are passed in peace and quietude, in the midst of fertile fields, surrounded by magnificent mountains, in a healthful climate. They have good horses and vehicles, good roads, great barns and haystacks, orchards loaded with fruit, hives full of honey, cattle on a thousand hills, flocks and herds in the mountain vales, and if they are not happy the fault lies not in their temporal condition.

SEVIER COUNTY.

This County lies south of Sanpete and is almost in the dead center o the Territory. Sevier Valley and one of its tributaries, Salina Creek, represent the greater part of its area. There are 45,106 acres of tillable land already, but this will be largely increased during the coming year from the 8000 acres set aside to the University fund. Sevier is an agricultural and stock raising district, although many varieties of mineral exist within its lines. Along the course of the Sevier River are a number of towns of some importance, and between them is a great extent of arable and cultivated land, all of which is irrigated, there being 206 miles of irrigating canals within the county. The land is extremely fertile, the usual cereals and grasses yielding well. Among the crops reported, some range as high as 82 bushels of wheat and 97 bushels of barley to the acre. In the southeastern portion of the county the mountains are high, but among the peaks are frequent plateaus of great extent, whose summer range for cattle is not excelled by any in the Territory. The scenery among these mountain ranges is not so wild as it becomes further south, and is relieved by the view of large stretches of timber and pasture land. The county is entered by the Rio Grande Western Railway, whose terminus is at Salina, and the people of this flourishing town, which is an important commercial point, count with confidence on its becoming an important point on a through railway. It is more than likely that a west bound line will make Salina a junction city, by virtue of Salina Canyon being a natural gateway between the east and the west. At this point the Wasatch Mountains may be crossed more easily than by any other pass, the grade being only one per cent. on one side and two on the other. The county has been well developed, considering its remoteness, and the assessed valuation for 1893 was $1,388,700 Building stone of excellent quality is said to abound in the foothills of the mountains, making it comparatively cheap for substantial homes to be built. The population is about 7,500. Richfield is the county seat, with 2000 people. Like nearly all of the other towns in the county, it is situated in the midst of a rich farming district. It is said to be located on the site of a prehistoric city, whose inhabitants were probably attracted by the warm medicinal springs which flow from the foothills. The town has two steam planing mills, a steam flouring mill and a grain elevator, besides other important buildings. Like many other southern towns, the streets are lined with shade trees and streams of mountain water. Another principal town in the county is Monroe, with its nice residences belonging to wealthy cattle and sheep owners, and its industrial enterprises. Salina, the terminus of the railway, is so called from the great beds of rock salt which exist in the neighborhood, and several salt works are engaged in a small way in this branch of manufacture. Good opportunities for further development exist in this direction. Mexican onyx, alum, coal and gypsum abound in the mountains near by. The streams in this county are well filled with trout and attract sportsmen in the summer season. A town in the southern part, Joseph, at the mouth of Clear Creek Canyon, where the soil is fertile and in the neighborhood of undeveloped mines of gold, silver and copper, has a large flouring mill, a small brass foundry, and a pork packing establishment. It is also supplied with water works and is altogether a delightful town. Glenwood, east of Richfield, is a little town which is proud of its water power, having two flouring mills, and an ambition to possess other manufacturing concerns. The chief interests at the present time are those that pertain to the range. Other towns are Redmond, Aurora, Sigurd, Central, Annabella and Burrville. At a place called Plateau a sanitarium was started two years ago, and a number of patients found great benefit in the soft, pure atmosphere of this mountain resort.

SUMMIT COUNTY.

BY "49ER."

This county lying east of Salt Lake County, embraces ten miles in length (from the Cottonwoods east) of the great mineral belt, on which is situated the Ontario, Daly, Anchor, Silver King, Crescent, West Daly, Morgan, Meears and many others that are considered paying mines, some of which have paid vast sums in dividends, and will do so again, when the present criminal discrimination against silver is at an end. There are more than 750 locations on record, most of them surveyed and patented in Uintah district. The limits of this pamphlet will not permit even the naming of the promising mining properties, that could be opened to employ thousands of men if politics and foreign influences would let us alone. Take for example the Ontario Mine. In twenty years it has taken $30,000,000. from the mines, and paid in dividends over $14,000,000. Its stock at fifteen dollars per share, on which it paid fifty cents monthly for eighteen years has yielded eighteen per cent. per annum, and built up a town of 3000 inhabitants, affording a market for the surrounding country, its timber, wood, coal, and supplies of all kinds. The pay roll monthly makes happy the better part of two and a large part of four counties. This belt runs along and is the dividing line between Summit and Wasatch Counties, the valleys of each being farming and grazing lands, dotted with ranches, producing hay, grain and vegetables, while the hills afford grazing ranges in summer for sheep, cattle, and horses. When these mines can be worked at their full capacity, and other properties opened up, they will afford a livelier market for the products of the surrounding country. A large part of the profits of this and other paying properties has been expended in development work upon hundreds of locations on the great belt, one-half of the entire output, or gross product having been expended in timber, roads, coal, hoisting and pumping machinery, mills, thousands of acres of timber, and everything that goes to make up a great plant, as complete in all its details as any in the United States. The clock-like regularity and uninterrupted industry of the whole plant, to put the ore into marketable bullion, has not been excelled. It is probable that several of the above named mines, and many not mentioned, will approach the Ontario as future developments progress. It is but just to the owners and superintendents of the Ontario, Daly, Silver King, Anchor and Crescent, to say that they are representative Americans, that in these stringent times they have not tried to reduce wages, and will keep running so long as expenses can be paid. The miners and community appreciate the fairness and sympathy of Messrs. Chambers, Daly, Keith, Emery, Kearns, McGregor and others of the camp, who have done their best to keep the mines open under adverse circumstances. There is nothing that pays like a paying mine. A man (like some in Mexico) may build up a family record 300 years old with princely revenues, that has cost only moderate prudence and tenacity to hold and enjoy. The mines of Summit and Wasatch Counties are not the only sources of revenue of these counties. Vast quarries of sandstone and brown stone, the most durable of building rocks, are found and being utilized in Salt Lake. The great coal veins of Summit County have been described in the chapter on the mineral resources of the Territory.

The following table will show what it takes to produce silver bullion, and for what silver dollars are distributed. The disbursements for the Ontario alone, for 1890 were as follows:

Payroll and Salaries,	$535,000 00
Cord Wood,	34,180 75
Lumber and Timber,	35,649.50
Coal from Coalville,	81,794.22
Salt,	29,662.82
Castings, Salt Lake Foundries,	12,867.10
Beef and Vegetables,	21,724 03
Hauling and Sampling Ore,	55,853.10
Sundries, Powder, Oil Mach., Candles, Groceries, etc. N. Y. and S. F. Offices,	310,323.54
Dividends, twelve of $75,000 each,	900,000 00
Total,	$2,017,055.06

Other mines distribute their money in about the same proportion. The benefits keep alive and build up whole communities Considering the aggregate of mines, however, and the hundreds of locations that do not pay, every dollar has cost more than 100 cents, but it has multiplied itself in its paying capacity, and is indestructible for all time. It is a dollar that floods, rats, and fire cannot destroy. Park City, Coalville, Wanship, Peoa, Kamas, Echo, and a number of villages contain the population of Summit County, which by no means depends entirely on its mineral resources. The assessed valuation is $4,157,296.00 which, of course, does not include the value of its mines. The agricultural lands lie along the courses of the Bear, Weber and Provo Rivers, and the yield per acre is heavy. The water supply is greater than will ever be used.

TOOELE COUNTY.

This county, lying west of Salt Lake County, was one of the first to be settled in the Territory. It is among the largest in area, but a great portion is absolutely desert and may never be of any value whatever. Strange to say, however, the desert lands are all set aside by themselves in the western part of the county, while the eastern half is as beautiful and fertile as any land the sun shines upon. In the lovely Tooele Valley, lying between the Oquirrh and Stansbury Mountains, are some 20,000 acres of tillable land, about half of which is cultivated and well watered, partly from mountain streams and partly from drive artesian wells, which yield abundantly in most parts of the valley. Cultivated land in this valley is worth as high as $75 per acre, but there are about 100,000 acres of tillable land in the county that has not been taken up. Among the chief farming products are wheat, which sometimes yields as high as eighty bushels to the acre; potatoes, running up to 400 bushels; lucern, fruit, etc. A considerable revenue is derived from the stock interests, wool, hides, beef and mutton being shipped in large quantities. Fruit is exceptionally fine in flavor, and the crops are large. Peaches yield as much as 300 bushels of handsome fruit to the acre. A fruit canning and evaporating concern could do well in Tooele City; and it has been suggested that a fruit distillery would pay, owing to the cheapness of the fruit and the large quantities that go to waste every season for want of a market. Among the other enterprises invited to Tooele County are a dairy and cheese making concern, and an electric light and power company, utilizing the water power of Tooele City, which has a fine system of water works. The region is extremely healthful and conducive to long life, and the beautiful scenery, with mountain, lake and islands in full view, make the eastern part of the county a very pleasant place to live in.

In the mineral history of Utah, Tooele County has played an important part, some of the richest viens ever found in the West having been among the first mines to be worked in the county. The celebrated Ophir district has contributed millions to the gold, silver and copper wealth of the nation. Some of the best properties of the Deep Creek region, in the extreme western part of the Territory, are also within its lines. But its treasure trove is now the greater part of the Mercur gold region, just coming into prominence as one of the most extraordinary discoveries of the age. Unlike the Deep Creek deposits, these have the advantage of being near the line of a great railway.

Garfield Beach, the great bathing resort of the Union Pacific, on the shore of Great Salt Lake, is in Tooele County, on the line of the Utah and Nevada Railway, whose terminus is near Grantsville.

The population of the county is about 5,000, and the assessed valuation $1,809,802, but with the Mercur developments these will both be greatly increased during the present year.

UINTAH COUNTY.

Uintah County covers a large area, but the greater portion of it is occupied by the Uintah and Uncompahgre reservations. The northern part of the county, however, along the valley of the Duchesne, is fertile and sustains a flourishing farming and trading population. The principal town is Vernal, and for a considerable distance east and west of this settlement, along the base of the lofty Uintah Mountains, the farming land is all taken up, and is yielding excellent crops, but the district open to settlement for such purposes is cut off on the south by the Indian reservations and on the north by the high mountains. These mountains afford a vast supply of timber, their northern flanks being the greatest forest region of the Territory. The scenic features of this county are not excelled by any in the Territory, although they are peculiar; the wonders consisting of the narrow rocky gorges through which the waters drain from the snowy peaks of the Uintah Mountains. The population of the county is about 4000. But for its remoteness from railroad communication the mining interests of this region would have received a great deal of attention. Gold, silver and lead ores are found in great quantity, and in the old Bullionville district is one of the greatest copper mines to be found in this country. This property is so vast and so rich that even located as it is, eastern parties have spent considerable money on its development, and the ore has been taken by wagons one hundred miles over the mountains to the railway, sent thence to Chicago, and profit realized on its shipment. The people of this county look forward to the day when a railway will traverse the valley of the Duchesne on its way from Colorado to Salt Lake City, in which case the wonderful resources of this region will soon become apparent. It is in Uintah County, near Fort Duchesne, that the large bodies of gilsonite or asphaltum have been found, and shipments have been made to the amount of hundreds of carloads to all the principal cities of the east, where it is in steady demand for the manufacture of varnish.

UTAH COUNTY.
BY D. R. CORAY.

This garden spot of Utah, in the center of the territory and in the central and most fertile part of the Great Basin, is not alone a garden, but the most beautiful district in all the mountain region. Utah Lake, its central gem, is bordered on every side by thousands of acres of richest farming land, while the towering peaks of the Wasatch and Oquirrh ranges form a background to it all. Scarcely any place on earth shows a fairer picture. It has a population of 30,000, and an area of 2124 square miles. The mountains occupy 1424 square miles, and the valley suitable for agriculture, 565 square miles. The area of Utah Lake is 155 miles. Of tillable land there are 342,400 acres, of which there is under cultivation 91,200 acres; 251,200 acres are capable of cultivation. The average elevation of the valleys above the sea is 4,500 to 4,800 feet; the highest mountain peak is 12,000 feet, being one of the highest peaks of the Wasatch range. The assessed valuation is $10,000,000. (Mines, irrigation properties, school property and mortgages are non-assessable.) The total valuation of developed mining property is $16,000,000; irrigation properties, $3,000,000. The average valuation per capita is $966.66. The county has no bonded indebtedness, but has municipal bonds of $125,000, and school bonds of $47,500. The county has 206.35 miles of standard guage railroad now in operation, traversing the county in every direction. The valuation of school property is $321,921.00.

Utah County has sixteen thriving cities and villages. *Provo*, the county-seat, is the largest, having a population of 6,000. It is beautifully situated on the east shore of Utah Lake, with broad streets' on either side of which flow clear streams of pure mountain water bordered with shade trees. A few hours drive takes one from the busy city into the grandest scenery in the Wasatch and the best trout fishing in the west. The scenery in the North Fork of the Provo River is unsurpassed anywhere, and Utah Lake invites the bathers on hot summer days. Provo is located on two transcontinental railways, the Rio Grande Western and the Union Pacific, and in all probability will be on the next transcontinental line that is built, as Provo Canyon is the best natural gateway through the Wasatch. To all of the valley of Utah Lake and the vast Territory of the South, Provo is the natural distributing point.

Public Institutions.—At Provo is located the Territorial Insane Asylum—erected at a cost of $300,000.00. The B. Y. Academy has a wide-spread reputation as a seat of learning. Most of its students come from other places. The Proctor Academy, controlled by the New West Educational Commission, is conducted on a regular academic plan.

Provo has a complete system of water works, and electric light and street car service.

CITIES AND TOWNS.

Lehi is a thriving town in the north end of the county with a population of 3,000. Its principal industry is the Lehi Sugar Works and it is the nearest town of any size to the Camp Floyd mining camp. It has a most efficient city government, and starts the year of 1894 without a dollar of indebtedness. Lehi is the junction of the Union Pacific and the Salt Lake and Western Railroads. The principal shipping products receive special mention hereafter.

Springville.—Six miles south of Provo, is a thriving, beautiful city of 2,500 people who have, for many years, kept the city "a prohibition town." It is on the Union Pacific Railroad, and is the junction of the Tintic Range and Rio Grande Western Railroad. Situated midway between and on the direct line of railroad between the iron and coal fields of Utah County, with splendid facilities as a manufacturing center, its future is assured.

Spanish Fork and Payson are each thriving centers of large agricultural districts, and are the principal points of shipment of agricultural products within the county.

First of Utah County's developed resources are her *Agricultural Products*, in which she is among the first in rank of Utah's counties. A brief summary is here given of her cultivated land and the most important products:

	Acres Cultivated.	Average yield per acre.	Highest yield per acre.	Average Price.
Wheat	11,000	30 bu.	60 bu.	$ .70 per bu.
Barley	8,125	32 "	76 "	.90 per cwt.
Oats	6,240	35 "	90 "	1.00 "
Rye	5,460	25 "	50 "	1.00 "
Sugar	2,200	13 tons	35 tons	5.00 per ton.
Orchard and vineyard	3,640			
Potatoes	3,000	300 bu.	840 bu.	.30 per bu.
Sorgum	650			
Buckwheat	600			
Flax	230			
Garden	2,100			
Alfalfa	23,790	4 tons	10 tons	5.00 per ton.
Tame and wild grasses	16,500	2 "	3½ "	7.00 "
Forest and Park	3,000			

Nearly all of the products are consumed within the Territory with the exception of barley, rye, potatoes and alfalfa. These find ready sale in the Eastern market, a higher price being paid for the barley and rye than for the Eastern prairie product. Large quantities of barley are shipped to Milwaukee, St. Louis and California, where it rates up to the best Canadian Brewing. Utah potatoes are known and in demand everywhere, while alfalfa finds a ready sale in all markets. Utah County wheat is a brighter, fuller kernal than the Eastern products *as all irrigation products are.* It grades as No. 2 red in the market, but little of it gets farther away than Colorado. The demand in the intermountain region exceeding production, it is all consumed at home. Spanish Fork produces more wheat than any other precinct in the county, and their yield is larger per acre principally for the reason that they have learned to use the water economically. Flax, sorgum and buckwheat are only produced in small quantities for home consumption.

Sugar Beet Industry.—The chief agricultural product at present is sugar beets. The crop for 1893, as received at the Lehi Sugar Factory, is estimated at 26,800 tons. The price paid at the factory was $5.00 per ton, or $135,000 for the entire crop. Work began in the early part of September and ended for the season in January. At the close of this season 26,800 tons of beets had been consumed, yielding 3,877,110 pounds of dry granulated sugar of first quality. The daily average of beets used was 305 tons, and the output of sugar 412 sacks of 98 pounds each. The totals of other materials consumed in the manufacture during the past season up to November 30th, were as follows: 4,676 tons of

The golden harvest, Provo Valley

coal and 1700 tons of limestone, which required 7328 bushels of coke to convert it into lime (all Utah County products). The factory is the largest in the United States, employing 150 regular working men, and the quality of the sugar produced has been attested by the awarding committee of the Columbian Exposition, which gave to it *the first prize*.

The great importance of the sugar enterprise, however, is more strikingly revealed in its agrarian feature. The average yield of the beets, after careful comparison, has been fixed at 13 tons per acre, with a maximum yield of 35 tons. To deliver the crop at the factory costs the farmer an average of 30 cents a ton. Out of the gross receipts of $65.00 per acre he therefore receives $61.10 per acre as the net proceeds of his labor from the present average crop. But in the difference between the average and the maximum crop appears a vast opening for improvement in the methods of cultivation. Moreover there is a like difference manifest in the amount of saccharine matter produced from a given quantity of beets. The average yield per ton of beets has been ascertained to be 130 pounds for the present season, while the largest quantity produced from one ton was 200 pounds.

It is manifest, then, by experiment in fertilizing and general tillage and in selection of land, a very much larger average may be reached than the one given; thus increasing the profit of both the farmer and manufacturer. The further fact that the present season is, in these respects, very much in advance of its predecessors, shows the high water mark in cultivation is near at hand. J. R. Jones, Lehi, reports having raised last year 127 tons of sugar-beets on four acres of land. A. J. Webb raised over 214 tons from ten acres, for which he received $1,072.25.

Orchard and *Vineyard* are considered together as to acreage, on account of their inseparability, because nearly every farmer's vineyard is a part of his orchard. Though occupying only one-third of the acreage, in the care given and in the value of its product, the vineyard stands far ahead, for many of the vineyards were only planted recently and every care has been given in culture and the planting of the best quality of grapes. The product is equal to the best California grapes. The orchards of the county are extensive, though but little cared for; when care is given them the yield is as large and the quality of the fruit as fine as any produced in the United States. One orchard of thirteen acres in the north end of the county has produced for the last five years an average of $10,000 per annum, and a great many other horticulturists have recently planted orchards varying in area from five to two hundred acres, with a prospect of ultimately attaining this same success. All kinds of apples, pears, peaches, plums, cherries, apricots and prunes grow here to perfection. Most of the product is consumed at home, the shipments at the present time amounting to not over twenty car loads per annum.

Utah County has 50 000 acres of as fine vineyard and fruit land as can be found anywhere, with a climate particularly adapted to the culture of the same.

Live Stock.—There are owned in the county at present something over 250,000 sheep. The average clip of Utah County sheep is seven pounds per fleece, making an annual production of 1,750,000 pounds of wool. Our factories only consume, at present, from 450,000 to 550,000 pounds of wool, leaving a surplus for shipment of 1,200,000 pounds. This, at the prices of 1891 and 1892, brought to the sheep raisers of the county for wool exported, $216,000. The manufactured woolen goods produced by the two woolen mills of the county, only using about one-fourth of the clip, sold for about $180,000; $250,000 is received annually for muttons shipped to Chicago; this gives an annual income from all the branches of the sheep industry $646,000. If all the wool was manufactured in the county this would amount to over $1,000,000 per annum.

There are owned in Utah County some 10,000 head of range cattle, and 6,500 head of milch cows. A small portion of our beef cattle find an eastern market though nearly all are consumed at home.

The milch cows play quite an important part in the good living of the residents of the county. There are creameries all over the county at a distance of about six miles from each other making a cash market for any surplus of milk. The pulp of the sugar beets, after the sugar has been extracted, is proving very satisfactory for the fattening of beef steers and is finding a ready market among feeders at a price of seventy-five cents per ton.

The county possesses horses and mules, 9,600, hogs, 3,600.

The Provo Woolen Mills.—The erection of the Provo Woolen Mills was commenced prior to 1870. The main building is a four-story stone structure, and is the largest woolen factory west of the Missouri River. It was built at a time when building material and machinery were very high; but, considering the fact that it was the first woolen mill built west of Chicago, has survived panics, has never been mortgaged, has paid dividends nearly every year, and has kept abreast of the times, the people of the county and territory look upon it with pride as the best object lesson of home manufacture. The mill is an eight set plant, employs 125 operatives and consumes 400,000 to 450,000 lbs. of wool annually. Its annual output brings the owners $125,000 to $150,000, exclusive of its electric light plant, which furnishes Provo City with light. The power is derived from a canal from Provo River, developing at the mills 100 horse power, with 5,000 cubic feet of water per minute over a 16 foot fall.

James Whitehead, Jr., of Springville, owns and operates a woolen mill of one-fourth the capacity of the Provo Woolen Mill, with proportionately the same results.

Undeveloped Resources.—The first and most important of these is the undeveloped farming lands of the county. These amount to 251,200 acres, that are a desert without irrigation, but with irrigation are as productive as any land that man ever put plow into; therefore the consideration of our water supply is necessary first. The streams of the county flowing into the Utah Lake basin, have an average annual flow of 1165 cubic feet of water per second, or over 36,510,000,000 cubic feet per annum, sufficient to irrigate 838,150 acres of land. Artesian water is found everywhere at depths varying from 25 to 200 feet, with good constant supply, and force enough to raise the water 20 feet above the surface—nearly every farm has one or more. In the county, only 91,200 acres are now irrigated, and the summer flow of the streams is claimed, but not used, in this irrigation and for power purposes. On two canals recently built the repairs are less than four per cent. Not many years hence Utah County will be as well and economically watered as any part of California. With water for 832,150 acres, and only 342,400 to water, we have an over-abundant supply. At present most of the water goes to waste, as it comes chiefly when the snow is melting in the early summer, but natural reservoirs exist upon the upper courses of all the streams and can be utilized at a small expense. As yet, development in this line is in its infancy. At only one point has anything been done, and that is by the Starr Irrigation Company, a home enterprise. This company is storing the waters of Currant Creek, and irrigating 25,000 acres of the fine lands of Goshen Valley. Their work is not completed, but their estimates show the total cost of the reservoir and canals will be less than $6.00 per acre for the lands irrigated. The dam, which stores 1,200,000,000 cubic feet of water, will cost only $10,000, is of solid masonry, and is built in a natural gateway to the upper valley, which is only 140 feet wide. It is only in the storage of large bodies of water that the cost per acre of irrigated land can be brought to the low figures given here, and it is impossible for one or a few farmers to do it, yet it gives the finest inducement to capital that can be found anywhere.

Next in importance to agriculture is the use of our water power for manufacturing purposes. Nine flouring mills, two woolen mills, four planing mills, three foundries and ten saw mills now use water as their motive power, and their combined plants represents 650 horse power.

Every stream in the county represents a vast source of undeveloped wealth in the power that a proper use of its water will furnish.

Utah County will in the near future develop and use this great power which at present is going to waste every day, the few manufactures already established here having fully demonstrated the fact that everything the entire people need and use can be manufactured cheaper and better here than to send our products east 2000 miles for manufacture and back for use, for Utah's wool crop alone furnishes employment for thousands of people in the far East who do not want our silver, and are keeping those who do want it from using it. In a short time our natural facilities will be developed; Utah will manufacture all she needs and the East cannot have our gold. The only way they could have kept our people tributary to them was to keep us digging in the hills instead of developing our natural resources; that they have refused to do, and the East can soon wear its own manufactured goods. A volume might be written on the undeveloped water power of Utah County and do no more than justice to its actual resources. Those who are interested, or wish to be, in manufacturing or power development in the inter-mountain region can come and see us, and we will take pleasure in showing you our power facilities, the finest trout fishing, with the grandest, most beautiful natural scenery, all on the same stream and within easy drive of our central and capital city, Provo.

Third in importance are the *Mines and Quarries* of which the following are found within the county; gold, silver, iron, lead, coal, asphaltum and bituminous limestone, ozokerite, slate, onyx, graphite, marble, granite, sandstone, antimony, cinnabar, sulphur, zinc, copper, serpentine, limestone and soda.

Utah County, while depending mainly on its agricultural resources, represents an immense field of mineral wealth, mostly undeveloped, and each year some great strike of ore in the mining districts turns the attention of her people to look for wealth in the mines and prospects. Up to the year 1893 silver has been the principal metal sought for, but the recent discoveries of gold in the Camp Floyd District together with the legislation against silver, has placed gold to the front in our metals. Gold is found in paying quantities at Camp Floyd in the form of a chloride, which can only be milled successfully by the cyanide process, at a cost of mining and milling of only $1.92 per ton of ore.

Camp Floyd Mining district is in Utah and Tooele Counties, about half of the present claims being in each county. The nearest railroad point is Fairfield on the Union Pacific, six miles from the mines. The principal mines now operated are the Mercur and the Marion Groups, the former of which is in Tooele and the latter in Utah County. The ore is low grade, running from $4.00 to $24.00 per ton, but is found in very large masses extending over an immense territory estimated at not less than 500 square miles, the larger portion of which is in Utah County. The most attractive feature of the mines is that the ores do not lie deep and pay almost from the surface. Mining for silver has been carried on in this district, for a number of years, but the gold discoveries are quite recent. The Mercur and some other mines have been known for over a year, but the knowledge was not general until late in 1893. In the coming spring it will be the most profitable field to work in in the West. There are about 500 men in the district working the claims already located, but conservative men estimate that many thousands will be working there within two years. The district now produces $60,000.00 per month in gold. The milling capacity at present is 120 tons per day.

Silver and lead is found in the mountains of Utah County in paying quantities on all sides, though the most productive mines are in the Tintic District, which is partly in Utah and partly in Juab Counties, comprising the great mines around Eureka and Silver City, among which, within the county, are the Sioux, Northern Spy, Bullion-Beck, Caresa, Tintic Tunnel Company, Utah Consolidated and Godiva, all dividend paying, and in the American Fork District which joins the Park City District of Summit County in which some great producing mines, as the Miller, Wild Dutchman and Pittsburg have been found.

The splendid *coal fields* of the county, are described under the head of mining. In Utah County near Tintic are situated vast *iron fields*, capable of furnishing millions of tons, so free in its nature that it is used as a flux by the smelters of Salt Lake Valley. The Utah Valley Iron Mining & Manufacturing Company, of which Mr. A. A. Noon of Provo, is president and manager, and to whose individual effort most of the present development is due, is the largest operator. The property consists of large bodies of iron ore less than thirty miles rom Provo City. The deposits extend over some 320 acres of ore, which is found in dikes. For mining the ore it is only necessary to clear off a light covering of earth, and then to quarry with drill and powder; the workings are nearly 100 feet high, but this is not the depth of the beds, for the floors of these quarries are of solid iron ore, and of the purest quality, reaching in the earth to unknown depths. Developments have been made in these deposits exposing such qualities of ore that it would be difficult to name a place where they are rivaled in extent or excellence of quality. The working of these bodies is inexpensive. The Rio Grande Western Railroad runs within six miles of the mines, and the wagon road from there to the mines is of easy grade; single teams can be driven to and from any part of them, and haul 6,000 pounds at a load. Many other deposits of excellent iron exist in the mountains in the southern part of the county.

Sandstone is the most important of our building materials, owing to its general excellence and cheapness. The deposits in this region are noteworthy for their great depth and almost uniform quality in texture and color. In texture they are so fine, close and tenacious as to retain the most delicate touches of the chisel, and can be turned in a lathe or planed. In resistance to pressure strains they range from 5,000 to 9,000 pounds to the cubic inch—a tenacity only exceeded by a few of the limestones, gneiss and granite.

Sandstone is principally quarried by the Kyune Graystone Company and Diamond, Kyune and Castle companies. The red sandstones are quarried at the Diamond Quarry near Thistle. The gray or kyune stone is found nine miles southeast of P. V. Junction on the R. G. W. Railway. Two extensive quarries have been opened near P. V. Junction and the ledge is apparently continuous between the two points. The sandstones of the kyune quarries are of a bluish-gray color, even texture, fine grain, freedom from iron and other elements, (being ninety-six per cent. pure silica,) freedom from stains and seams, regularity of tint throughout the ledge, (an important element where a large building would require the same tint throughout,) and also in the enormous blocks that may be quarried without a blemish or a crack to injure its strength.

The above characteristics apply both to the grey and red sandstone, with the addition that the latter has greater resisting power, due to the cementing quality of the iron sesqui-oxide which it contains, and which also imparts the red color. In a commercial sense this stone is more valuable than the grey, owing to its comparative rarity in large masses and the great demand for it by the builders throughout the country. The tendency among architects today is towards liveliness in style and contrasts in color, which impels the use of highly tinted materials, if only in the trimmings, and our red sandstone quarries present every shade, from pale salmon to rich purple-brown. Large deposits of really good red stone are rare, most of the stone of good quality being more brown than red. The stone lies in several natural cleavage beds from one to twenty feet in thickness and can be quarried in blocks of any size. It splits perfectly and regularly in any direction.

This stone is largely used now in the finest buildings in the Territory, some of the best buildings in Salt Lake City being built entirely of it, while it is much used for fronts and trimmings everywhere. Its use has already spread outside of the Territory. The Yesler building, Seattle, H. W. Corbett's Block, Portland, and the residence of Col. D. C. Dodge, Denver, are the principal foreign buildings.

The annual product of the quarries for 1893 was 1,900 cars. The quarries employ 185 men.

Utah County furnishes most of the *Mexican Onyx* shipped from the Territory, the principal deposits being on the west shore of Utah Lake, about fifteen miles from Provo and the same distance from Lehi. The beds were first discovered by Professor Cedarstrom who lives near them and to whose individual efforts we are mainly indebted for its present development.

Two companies are now developing the deposits, and if they continue as well as the indications foreshadow, large sawing and polishing plants will be in operation in this vicinity by another year.

Onyx is also found in many places on the east side of Utah Lake, the deposits being at about the same elevation above the lake and evidently formed under the same conditions. The Devey and Wadley claims, near Pleasant Grove, are a series of caves extending over three miles. These caves contain onyx of almost every variety of color and shade. The largest of these caves is 300 feet wide and 200 feet deep. These mines are easy of access and have furnished two carloads of onyx for the state capital at Denver.

Asphaltum—The deposits of asphaltic limestone and bituminous rock are of immense extent, being found in large beds over an extent of one hundred square miles within the county: and while these forms of asphaltum are found in many places in Utah, the only real development has been in Utah County. Asphaltic limestone and bituminous rock are largely mined for paving purposes, and for that reason have been fully developed. It has been used quite extensively in St. Louis, Denver and Salt Lake for that purpose. Parties connected with the Anheuser Brewing Company of St. Louis, own one of the largest alphaltum mines and have spent considerable sums in their development. The Wasatch Asphaltum Company, of Salt Lake City, have also expended $80,000 in developing their mines, and in the erection of plants for the treatment of the rock Their paving plant in Salt Lake City is one of the largest and best in the United States.

This company is engaged in producing asphaltic limestone from its mines near Clear Creek station, on the line of the Rio Grande Western Railway, and preparing it for use at its mills in Salt Lake City. The deposit is the only one of its kind found in economic quantity in the United States, and the material as mined resembles very closely that from the Val de Travers, Switzerland, which for a whole generation has been acknowledged the finest asphaltum for paving purposes the world has produced. It has been in use during the last twenty years in Paris and London and other large European cities, and has stood the test of time and wear to the satisfaction of every civil engineer who has examined it. The mines of the Wasatch Asphaltum Company are the first to produce for market a grade of asphaltic limestone in America of the same character as those of Switzerland; but the product of these Utah mines runs higher in its percentage of asphaltum than that of Europe. This company is undoubtedly offering the finest asphaltic limestone in the world. Every citizen of the United States may well take pride that America is now producing a mineral that has hitherto been imported from Europe, and Utah County has the honor of having the deposit within its borders. The mines being of great extent, the quantity is practically unlimited. Asphaltic limestone is absolutely imperishable, as it contains no ingredient that is volatile under 300 degrees F., and it is not subject to any atmospheric changes Its wearing qualities are unsurpassed. Notwithstanding the high character of this paving material, the Wasatch Asphaltum Company has found it possible to produce and prepare it with such economy that it can be delivered in all parts of the United States, at a price that will justify its general use. Low rates of freight on asphaltum in carload lots enables the product to be put on the markets of the East at reasonable terms.

Deposits of ozokerite or mineral wax exist in Utah County, the principal development having been made by the New York Ozokerite Company, Mr. R. J. Kroupa, of Provo, general superintendent. The mines are on the line of the Rio Grande Western Railway at Soldier Summit, from which point shipments have been made.

Slate is found in large quantities in Slate Canyon, two miles east of Provo. The mines are four miles from the depot of both the R. G. W. and U. P. Railroads at Provo. Considerable development has been made, two mines having been opened up, producing mercantile roofing slate. The mines have only been recently developed, but the product last year was about five carloads of roofing material. They are of sufficient extent to furnish all the slate used in the West. All the development has been done by a few local men, without capital, and has necessarily been slow, as a road had to be constructed at considerable expense. This has been done and a good wagon road now connects the mines with the railroads. The present capacity of the quarries is forty squares of mercantile slate per day. Utah County has an exhibit of slate at the Midwinter Fair. Serpentine is found between the upper and lower slate beds in Slate Canyon, in large quantities. The quarries have not as yet been developed sufficiently to show their commercial value.

Marble exists at various points within the county, the quality being superior to the Tennessee, and equal to the best Vermont and European. The various beds furnish all grades and colors, pure white and red in layers, green and white and red in layers, mottled and black. The white and black are found in the vicinity of Lehi, and the colored varieties in Spanish Fork Canyon, near Thistle, on the R.G.W. Railway, at which point the beds cover an area of forty acres or more. The principal use up to the present time has been for ornaments, statuary and tombstones; but when our cities can afford that class of building material it will be more extensively used. Marble is also found in the mountains east of Springville, but the quarries are as yet undeveloped.

Graphite is found in considerable quantities in the hills on the east side of Utah Lake valley, from the north end of the county south to Spanish Fork Canyon, a distance of thirty miles. It is found principally in the form known as amorphous carbon and has been little developed, the principal uses up to the present time being for foundry facings, kiln and furnace linings, and most of it used has been taken from the hills just east of Provo. When the iron interests are developed, the graphite beds will be of great value. So extensive are the deposits in proportion to the present demands that none are considered of any particular value. Everyone goes and gets what he wants.

Nitre or *Saltpetre* is found in large quantities in the south end of the county. The deposits have never been developed, but in the early history of the Territory, during the Indian trouble and before the building of the Pacific Railway it was used quite extensively in the manufacture of gunpowder. After that the deposits were neglected until the year 1893 when a number of claims were located and partially developed. The principal deposits are located on Currant Creek near the village of Goshen where they are easily accessible and may in the near future furnish employment to a large number of men; as in spite of their long neglect these deposits should be among the most valuable in the country. Saltpetre is also found in considerable quantity in Spanish Fork Canyon.

Soda is found in considerable quantities in an almost pure state, at Pelican Point on the west shore of Utah Lake, about fifteen miles from Lehi, where the deposits are made from the waters of several springs which here rise along the shore of the lake. These deposits have been known for a number of years and a large amount of soda has been shipped from them, though it is fifteen miles to the nearest railroad point.

Granite and *Limestone* are found everywhere. Our mountains are composed of them, and they are largely used in our buildings. The quality of the limestones is far behind that of the sandstones for building purposes, and the cost of quarrying and cutting the granite is too great to admit of their general use.

Antimony, Cinnabar, Sulphur, Zinc and *Copper* are found at various points within the county. Some of them have been found in considerable quantities in connection with other minerals, but no paying mines have as yet been worked.

WASATCH COUNTY.

The greater part of this county in the northeastern part of the Territory is occupied by the Uintah Indian Reservation, which cuts out from settlement and occupation, one of the best watered and fertile regions of the Territory. Only a couple of hundred square miles have remained for occupation by the whites, and these are almost wholly in Provo Valley, a beautiful elevated tract, traversed by the Provo River and some of its important tributaries. From a scenic point of view, Provo Valley is as grand as any in Utah, the Wasatch Mountains with their snowy peaks, towering along the western side of the vale. Heber, Midway, Charleston and Wallsburgh are the only towns in the county, the population being about 5,000. Provo Valley is too high for fruit raising, but does well with wheat, oats and other crops. The assessed valuation of the county is $1,106,588, but this is exclusive of its mining interests, which are very important, as the county adjoins Summit and takes in a portion of the great mineral belt on which the Ontario and other famous mines are located. The character of the ores is similar to those of Summit County, although copper is more abundant. Zinc-blende and oxides of zinc are in vast quantities, mixed with lead and silver. Although widely prospected, the mines have not been opened in Wasatch County to such extent as those near Park City; but Snake Creek district has over 200 locations, many of them patented. A part of Blue Ledge district also lies in Wasatch County, and this has over 250 locations. The Park City mines have contributed largely to the support of the farming population of Wasatch County, and during all the period of Park City's prosperity, high prices have been secured throughout Provo Valley for every description of farming produce, while many of its towns-people have been employed in the mountains in the production of timber and other supplies for the mines. Some of the big cattle owners of the Territory live in Wasatch County, and in the event of the opening up of the Indian Reservation, this will prove to be one of the most important counties of the Territory. In the southern part of the county there is a region exempt from the reservation, but it is wild and mountainous and consists mostly of bad lands. Yet. h..e a variety of hydro-carbon deposits have been found, and among them the famous mines operated by the Salt Lake Gilsonite Company, from which is produced a large proportion of the gilsonite and pure gum asphaltum of such value that it will bear a seventy-five mile wagon haul to Price Station, and thence be profitably transported to the eastern markets for the manufacture of varnish. and for other purposes.

WASHINGTON COUNTY AND SOUTHERN UTAH

A desire for definite information relative to southern Utah, has for some time been shown, notably by the Nevada Southern Railway Company, and the Salt Lake Chamber of Commerce. To elicit the desired facts, public meetings have been held in St. George. the county seat of Washington County, and these brought about the orgaization of a committee on statistics, with sub-committees on agriculture, horticulture, stockraising, mining, and on merchandising and freight business; the sub-committees to report to the committee on statistics. The result of their labors so far is as follows:

Agriculture and Horticulture.—On the route between Muddy Valley, Nevada and Cedar City, Utah, there are twenty-one settlements on the line of travel, having a population of from six to seven thousand, with 10,320 acres under cultivation, and 8,130 acres being brought under cultivation. The cultivated land averages not less than twenty-five bushels of grain per acre, and in one settlement the average yield has been as high as thirty-eight bushels, while alfalfa shows an average of five tons per acre. This estimate does not include land to be irrigated by prospective reservoirs which will bring thousands of acres under cultivation.

Horticulture.—The climate and soil south of the "Rim of the Basin" is admirably adapted to the production of all kinds of peaches, nectarines almonds, plums, apples, pears, grapes, figs, pomegranates and other fruits. A large per cent. of what is now produced, however, goes to waste, for lack of transportation facilities. The county is also well adapted to the growth of all kinds of early garden stuff, such as radishes, lettuce, asparagus, celery, tomatoes, beans, cucumbers, melons, onions and Irish and sweet potatoes; also flowers of the choicest varieties, many of which are now blooming in December. In the settlements along the Rio Virgen and Lower Santa Clara Rivers the season for out-door gardening begins in the latter part of January, or the beginning of February. The climate of St. George and vicinity, with its delightful winters, often without a flake of snow, except what can be seen on the distant mountains, is unexceptionally healthful.

Stockraising.—This industry has chiefly been considered in the matter of exports, and the figures given are for those parts of Southern Utah, Northern Arizona and Southeastern Nevada, which would furnish freight to a line passing through St George. The report of 1894 estimates that 30,000 steers, 5,000 horses, 50,000 sheep, and 1,250,000 pounds of wool have been exported by the railroad.

Mining.—The advent of a railroad to St. George would make Southern Utah one of the richest sections in this inter-mountain country. There is an abundance of coal, iron, copper, gold, silver and lead ores, sulphur, ochre, alum, gypsum, mineral wax, and many other minerals, but the lack of cheap transportation makes it almost impossible to develop these prospects. Valuable properties that would yield millions if they could be properly worked are now lying idle. In Washington County 497 mining locations have been recorded. Silver Reef, the great southern camp has been one of the greatest mining agents toward the building up of Southern Utah, but for the last few years it has been quiet, and there is little hope for much progress unless silver becomes more valuable and easy transportation is accomplished. All the work done there now is by Chloriders. There are millions yet lying in the white sandstone of that region, and the Bull Valley Mining District contains vast bodies of low grade ore, gold, silver, lead, iron and copper, which cannot be worked with profit at present, because of freight rates and long hauls. A large amount of prospecting has been done, but work has been temporarily abandoned on account of so many difficulties. In the event of a railroad being built this Bull Valley country would become one of the largest mining camps in the West. In Tutsegavit Mining District, eighteen miles from St. George, are a large number of mining prospects owned and operated by the Dixie Mining and Smelting Company. The Apex and Morning Star, two of this group, are best described by a quotation from a report made by Mr. T. C. Williams, an expert sent out by an English company to negotiate for the purchase of the property. He says: "I consider from my examination of the mines that there are fully one hundred and fifty thousand, and probably two hundred thousand tons of ore in place at present, that will yield a net profit of not less than ten dollars, and probably more, per ton, basing the calculation upon the present methods employed in mining and marketing the product of the mine. I further believe that the mine at this writing is in shape to put out from sixty to one hundred tons per day of ore that will yield the above named profit of ten dollars per ton."

Situated about one mile west of the Dixie group and in the same chain of mountains, is the Mammoth Mine in which was struck a large cave filled with high grade carbonate ore, carrying from twelve to twenty-five ounces of silver. The Mountain Chief Mining Company, some years ago, ran a tunnel over one hundred feet in the Black Warrior Mine and struck a large body of carbonate of lead and silver. The company erected a smelter on the Santa Clara River, but high freight and long hauls ate up the proceeds and this property is not being worked at present. The St. George Mining Company, owns several fine prospects near the Dixie group and Mammoth claims, doubtless of equal value to the one referred to by Mr. Williams.

The Adams Lode in Bentley Mining District, about 45 miles from St. George, is owned by the Grand Gulch Mining Co. From this property about three hundred tons of ninety per cent. copper has been made and shipped, but again the long haul by wagon to the railroad has killed the enterprise. The mine, however, is an immense deposit, with ore all over the surface. Ores will average forty per cent. copper with twenty-five ounces of silver to the ton of copper, and many thousands of tons can be mined in open works, like quarrying stone for building purposes. Five miles east of this claim is the Savannic Mine, another large body of the finest copper ore. Near this property is the Cunningham Mine, which resembles the other two claims, and will be a great yielder when easy transportation is established. Any of these last named mines would bear a fifty-mile wagon haul. It was considered useless to put up works or spend much money on the Savannic or Cunningham mines, as the long wagon haul to the distant railroad made any attempt toward financial success impossible.

Situated about 25 miles east of the Grand Gulch property is the Copper Mountain Mining District, from which nearly fifty tons of copper bullion have been obtained; but the same complaint of long hauls and a decline in the price of the product has caused the abandonment of the effort. There are immense deposits of ore in the Red Bud and Red Cloud claims, which are located some 25 miles from St. George, and ten miles nearer the city in the Bentley District, is the Lynx or Hoot Owl Mine, which, though it has been worked but little, yields ore which is fifteen to forty per cent copper.

Upon the same road and from twelve to twenty miles from St. George, is situated some of the largest bodies of gypsum known. The deposit is fifty or more feet in thickness, and miles in length, is of the clearest and finest quality, and is so sound that it can be used for alabaster.

Northwest of St. George, at a distance of about twenty miles, is a ledge of iron ore twenty feet thick, running for miles; and near this are a number of antimony ledges of immense quantity and excellent quality.

Notwithstanding the difficulties of transportation, the Dixie Mining and Smelting Company have shipped 327,111 pounds of copper ore to the railroad at Milford 115 miles from St. George; also 101,722 pounds of copper matte, and 1,523 666 pounds of copper bullion, smelted at St. George with coke shipped in from Colorado. The copper as well as the silver lead ores of this section, are principally carbonate and are in great demand at all smelters for fluxing purposes.

Mercantile business.—In the event of a railroad passing through St. George, the following other cities, towns and villages would receive and ship freight by it. Washington, Price, Santa Clara, Pine Valley, Gunlock. Leeds, Harrisburg, Toquerville, Virgen City, Silver Reef, Duncan, Grafton, Rockville, Spring Dale, Shonesburg, Kanab, Orderville, Mount Carmel, Glendale, Upper Kanab, Johnson and Fredonia. A careful estimate shows that the merchants of these towns have shipped by the Union Pacific and Denver and Rio Grande Railroads for the year 1892 about twelve million pounds and have paid for freight about $120,000.00, in addition to an amount equally as large paid for team freight to and from the terminus at Milford. It is but fair to presume that freight business would be immensely increased by railroad facilities, and the consequent development of the resources of this region.

WAYNE COUNTY.

This county is situated in central southern Utah; watered by the Fremont River. It was the last county to be created in the Territory. About 10,000 acres are under cultivation, but this can be doubled by taking advantage of the opportunities for water that exist. Much tillable land is open for settlement, and cultivated farms with water-right and title can be had at present, at from $80 to $20 per acre. Although settlement was recent, a great variety of products have been developed. Of the leading farming crops are sheep, wool, lumber, orchard products, etc. Oats yield sixty bushels to the acre, wheat fifty bushels, potatoes 650 bushels, and hay six tons to the acre. Mineral resources are varied; gold, silver and copper, great deposits of pure gypsum, sulphur and bituminous shale, while stone coal is found in a number of localities in different parts of the county. It is a fine place for fishing and hunting; the climate is delightful, the winters mild and summers cool. It is an ideal fruit country. They already have lumber and flour mills, with plenty of timber in the mountains, cedar and pine. The population is only about 1000, but is rapidly increasing.

WEBER COUNTY.

This county, the second in wealth and population in Utah, contains 500 square miles, and is diversified by mountain and valley, affording fine grazing land for horses, cattle and sheep in the mountain districts, and the valley lands are the richest in Utah, comprising as they do almost 200 square miles of Great Salt Lake Valley, lying between the Wasatch Mountains and the shore of Great Salt Lake and watered by canals taken out from Ogden and Weber Rivers, and other canals supplied from the springs rising in the valley. East of the Wasatch Range, and in the eastern part of the county, lies Ogden Valley, six miles wide and twelve miles long, rich and fertile, but as it is much higher than Salt Lake Valley, therefore not so well adapted to the raising of fruit. The natural wealth of Weber County may be divided up as follows: agriculture, horticulture, grazing or stock-raising, mines and mining, and great natural advantages of water power and favorable location for manufacture.

In agriculture there has been uninterrupted success for forty years in the production of wheat, rye, oats, barley, corn, potatoes, cabbage, turnips, sugar beets, carrots, mangel-wurzel, sugar cane, celery, onions, tomatoes, cucumbers and every other product of the field or garden. Flax, hemp, timothy hay, blue grass, lucerne, red top and clover thrive as in few places on the earth.

Fruits.—All that the temperate regions of the earth produce thrive here— apples, peaches, plums, greengages, prunes, apricots, Siberian crab apples, cherries, currants, pears, quinces, grapes of many kinds, strawberries, blackberries, gooseberries, all of excellent quality, and from the above fruits the revenue to the inhabitants of the county is immense every year. There lies a great future for the county in the production of fruit. The proper attention has not been given to it of late years, otherwise the income would be about five-fold what it is at present. In the production of prunes alone there is no part of the United States better adapted to the growth of them than along the bench lands that skirt the Wasatch Mountains. The long, dry and warm season, with a clear sky throughout the entire summer, is well adapted to the proper curing of the prune, and at present 20,000 acres might be taken up and devoted to the production of this fruit. It would find a ready market north and east. The cultivation of the pear, apple, peach, cherry and apricot is carried on, and these fruits can be produced here in greater quantity per tree than anywhere in the inter-mountain region, and the number of railroads centering at Ogden, always will ensure a good market for such fruits.

Grazing.—A great part of the area of Weber County is devoted to grazing horses, cattle and sheep. A rich bunch grass covers the sides of the high mountains and waste lands of the valleys, and on this the stockman's herds fatten throughout the year. The beef and mutton they produce are of the best and the wool clip from the vast flocks of sheep is immense. Cattle, hogs, horses, sheep and goats are abundant. The value of these in Weber County reaches millions of dollars at present, and there is much land yet that may be made profitable by placing new herds thereon.

Mines and Mining.—The attention of the inhabitants has not been turned to the development of mines in this county as in other counties farther south, still the mineral wealth of Weber County is great. Gold, silver, lead, copper and zinc are found in the Wasatch Mountains east of Ogden, and iron is found in immense quantities at many places near Ogden. It is of the most superior quality; consisting of limonite, hematite, specular, magnetic and chromictery of iron equal to any found in the world, and in quantity they are practically inexhaustible. Some years since, at Ogden, works were established, and iron of the most superior brand was produced. As there is excellent limestone for fluxing, these are advantages which in the near future insure the erection in the county of extensive iron works and rolling mills for the production of steel rails and boiler plate. Along the shores of the lake soda is abundant, and from the saline waters of the lake millions of tons of salt may be produced annually. Saltpetre or nitrate of potash is abundant on the south fork of Ogden River. It is in a very pure state and much of it ready to use in the manufacture of gun powder.

Alum and Aluminum clays are found in immense quantities. East of Hot Springs, north of Ogden, and in the eastern part of the county, there are various measures of superior coal. Potters' clay of unsurpassed fineness is found in a stratum thirty feet thick, underlying the city of Ogden, and glass sand unequalled in America is found in vast beds west of Ogden.

Natural Gas is found by sinking at almost any point between the city of Ogden, and the shores of Salt Lake.

Slate, the like of which is found nowhere else west of Pennsylvania, is found in Taylor's Canyon. Granite, limestone, jasper, sandstone, oolitic limestone and soapstone, are found in quantities sufficient for any of the wants of man. Mica abounds in the hills east of Ogden, and a precious serpentine exists in Ogden Valley.

Population—The population of Weber County numbers 35,000 souls. Of these 22,500 live in the city of Ogden, The rest are distributed over the vast area of farming and grazing lands and also in Plain City, Hooper, Eden, Huntsville, Liberty, Harrisville, Marriotsville, North Ogden, Uintah and Riverdale. Ogden, the county seat of Weber County, Utah, is situated at the west base of Wasatch Mountains, and from the beautiful slope on which it rests, it overlooks Great Salt Lake and its many islands. With a thrifty population 22,500 souls and with paved streets, electric street-car lines, perfect sewerage, superior water supply and an excellent climate, it is at once the Mecca of the man who wants a home and happy bourne of him who seeks for health.

Ogden is the greatest railroad center at present west of Chicago. The Union Pacific, Utah Northern, Central Pacific, Utah Southern, Rio Grande Western railroads, the Ogden and Park City Railway and the Ogden and Hot Springs Road all center here. The grand union passenger depot receives the travel and traffic of these roads and is the handsomest building of its kind west of Chicago. On the first day of the present year the Southern Pacific Railroad Company opened its magnificent new machine repair and car shops in Ogden and these are to be increased by the addition of roller mills in the near future. Others of the railroads here now are preparing for the erection of equally fine shops. The Chicago and Northwestern Railroad now at Fort Casper is going to make Ogden its next objective point and at this point it will erect its machine and repair shops. The railroad now being built from Blake, California, on the Atlantic and Pacific, will make Ogden its northern terminus. Thus we see the natural center occupied by this city.

Its site is a beautiful one. It is watered by the Ogden and Weber rivers that flow through the city, the pure, crystal, cold waters of which take their birth in the virgin snows that crown the high peaks of the Wasatch Mountains. The water supply is inexhaustible and ample for a population of 200,000 souls. The system of supply is by a gravity fall of 200 feet, rendering it thereby inexpensive and perfect. Along with this water system owned by the Bear River Canal and Irrigation Company, there exists a water recourse known as the Bench Canal, carrying sufficient water for a possible increase of 200,000 inhabitants. The situation of Ogden is a most beautiful one, the high peaks, clad with perpetual snow, above it, and to the west the great Salt Lake Valley and broad expanse of the lake and its many islands. The climate is bracing and healthful, and added to this the Utah Hot Springs, a few miles north of the city, constitute the best Sanitarium in Utah.

The city is well built—there are private residences that would be an ornament to New York City. Fine churches owned by Mormons, Methodists, Catholics, Baptists, Episcopals, Unitarians and Agnostics. There are fine denominational schools, a convent school under the care of the Sisters of the Holy Cross. The building costing almost a quarter of a million dollars.

City Hall Square.

Ogden.
The Inter-Mountain Queen City.

The public school system is perfect, and the school houses are of a style of architecture equal to those of any city west of Chicago The school attendance is large, and the results of educational work are most creditable to the Board of Education.

There are six banks, each doing a good business, and the departments of trade are each and every one prosperous. In manufactures and industries, there are fruit canneries, pickling works, soap factories, flour mills, slaughtering establishments, a brick manufactory, founderies and bottling works. There is also an armory, the products and inventions of which reach into almost every country of the world.

One of the great forces destined to work for Ogden's future greatness is the tremendous water power afforded by the two rivers, the Weber and the Ogden.   From these two streams 21,000 horse power may be produced, destined to supply heat, light and motive power for every class of machinery for centuries to come.

As to history, Weber County may claim much that is interesting to the historian and the archæologist. Within her confines we find remains of the ancient race that antedates the Indian braves. Their mounds and writings are found along Ogden River, and near the towns. On Fremont Island, in Salt Lake, but within the line of the county, General Fremont discovered on his first expedition in the year 1843. at the north end of the island bearing his name, a cross and the date 1593, which proves that the early Spaniards under either Coronado or Cabesa de Vacca visited this region on a journey of exploration and discovery. During the last century, the site of Ogden was the trading ground of the Spanish and French troopers, and the agents of the Hudson Bay Company opened a post near the present forks of Ogden and Weber Rivers. The interests of this post were watched over by one, John Ogden, after whom the mountain overhanging the present city, the river and the valley above are named. This was about the year 1785 or 1790. and for many years after this man traded with the Shoshone, Bannock and Ute Indians of these regions.

In and along both rivers and by the mountain streams flowing into the lake, beaver and other fur-bearing animals were abundant. These afforded, for fifty years, a rich hunting ground to the troopers of the various companies whose partisans rambled over these regions.

In 1833 a band of troopers belonging to the American Fur Company visited this region. They were part of the expedition commanded by Captain Bonneville then on his way to the northwest coast of Oregon. Captain Bonneville remained at Soda Springs in Idaho, and sent forward this smaller expedition to go overland to Monterey on the coast of California for the purpose of exploration, and also to sell goods to the Spaniards. The Monterey expedition fared well enough until they reached the present site of Ogden City, where they encountered a band of Goshoot Indians, and a difficulty arose about a gun which had been stolen by the Indians from the troopers' camp. A fight ensued which ended in a total massacre of the entire Indian village, old and young, to the number of about forty persons. This massacre took place, it is supposed, about where the Reform School now stands, in the northeastern part of Ogden City. The white troopers passed on, reaching Monterey and returned in safety.

The next white man of whom we learn as holding power here was one, Mr. Goodyear, who took possession of the abandoned post of the Hudson Bay Company. He held possession here when the Mormons came in 1847, and sold what now constitutes almost the entire area of Weber County for the sum of $1800 to a Mr. William Brown who purchased the district for a Mormon colony, and as such it became at once a conspicuous little place. A mud wall six feet high was reared around a square that was a mile on each side, and for twenty years the little hamlet was an isolated spot through which the trains of emigrants on their way to Oregon or California passed and broke the dull monotony of peaceful life. The city wall has long since disappeared.

In the year 1868, when the Union Pacific Railroad came into Utah, it reached Ogden, and being thus left on the great highway of nations, the city's future became certain and its destiny assured. Since then its progress has been regular; and from a small adobe village of 500 souls, it has reached the position of second city in Utah.

In all its past history there was but one fatal error committed by its people, and that was that they did not reach out after and hold a part of the mining trade and reduction of ores from the mines of the south and west. This, however, her people hope to gain in the future, and as Ogden now stands her prospects are of the brightest. Her people are progressive, intelligent and determined. In the face of the present black cloud that hangs over the business of the world, her people have pushed ahead, believing in the future of their city, and when prosperity returns to our nation and the blessing of self-government rests upon Utah, Ogden will be one of the brightest stars in Utah's crown.

www.ingramcontent.com/pod-product-compliance
Lightning Source LLC
Chambersburg PA
CBHW031122160426
43192CB00008B/1082